WORLD HISTORY SERIES

Pirates

Titles in the World History Series

Pirates

by
Stephen Currie

Lucent Books, P.O. Box 289011, San Diego, CA 92198-9011

Library of Congress Cataloging-in-Publication Data

Currie, Stephen, 1960–
     Pirates / by Stephen Currie.
          p.   cm. — (World history series)
     Includes bibliographical references (p.) and index.
     ISBN 1-56006-807-8 (lib. : alk. paper)
     1. Pirates—Juvenile literature [1. Pirates.] I. Title. II. Series.
     G535.C87 2001
910.4'5—dc21   00-010394

Copyright 2001 by Lucent Books, Inc., P.O. Box 289011,
San Diego, California 92198-9011

Printed in the U.S.A.

Contents

Foreword

Each year on the first day of school, nearly every history teacher faces the task of explaining why his or her students should study history. One logical answer to this question is that exploring what happened in our past explains how the things we often take for granted—our customs, ideas, and institutions—came to be. As statesman and historian Winston Churchill put it, "Every nation or group of nations has its own tale to tell. Knowledge of the trials and struggles is necessary to all who would comprehend the problems, perils, challenges, and opportunities which confront us today." Thus, a study of history puts modern ideas and institutions in perspective. For example, though the founders of the United States were talented and creative thinkers, they clearly did not invent the concept of democracy. Instead, they adapted some democratic ideas that had originated in ancient Greece and with which the Romans, the British, and others had experimented. An exploration of these cultures, then, reveals their very real connection to us through institutions that continue to shape our daily lives.

Another reason often given for studying history is the idea that lessons exist in the past from which contemporary societies can benefit and learn. This idea, although controversial, has always been an intriguing one for historians. Those who agree that society can benefit from the past often quote philosopher George Santayana's famous statement, "Those who cannot remember the past are condemned to repeat it." Historians who subscribe to Santayana's philosophy believe that, for example, studying the events that led up to the major world wars or other significant historical events would allow society to chart a different and more favorable course in the future.

Just as difficult as convincing students to realize the importance of studying history is the search for useful and interesting supplementary materials that present historical events in a context that can be easily understood. The volumes in Lucent Books' World History Series attempt to present a broad, balanced, and penetrating view of the march of history. Ancient Egypt's important wars and rulers, for example, are presented against the rich and colorful backdrop of Egyptian religious, social, and cultural developments. The series engages the reader by enhancing historical events with these cultural contexts. For example, in *Ancient Greece*, the text covers the role of women in that society. Slavery is discussed in *The Roman Empire*, as well as how slaves earned their freedom. The numerous and varied aspects of everyday life in these and other societies are explored in each volume of the series. Additionally, the series covers the major political, cultural, and philosophical ideas as the torch of civilization is passed from ancient Mesopotamia and Egypt, through Greece, Rome, Medieval Europe, and other world cultures, to the modern day.

The material in the series is formatted in a thorough, precise, and organized manner. Each volume offers the reader a comprehensive and clearly written overview of an important historical event or period. The topic under discussion is placed in a broad, historical context. For example, The Italian Renaissance begins with a discussion of the High Middle Ages and the loss of central control that allowed certain Italian cities to develop artistically. The book ends by looking forward to the Reformation and interpreting the societal changes that grew out of the Renaissance. Thus, students are not only involved in an historical era, but also enveloped by the events leading up to that era and the events following it.

One important and unique feature in the World History Series is the primary and secondary source quotations that richly supplement each volume. These quotes are useful in a number of ways. First, they allow students access to sources they would not normally be exposed to because of the difficulty and obscurity of the original source. The quotations range from interesting anecdotes to farsighted cultural perspectives and are drawn from historical witnesses both past and present. Second, the quotes demonstrate how and where historians themselves derive their information on the past as they strive to reach a consensus on historical events. Lastly, all of the quotes are footnoted, familiarizing students with the citation process and allowing them to verify quotes and/or look up the original source if the quote piques their interest.

Finally, the books in the World History Series provide a detailed launching point for further research. Each book contains a bibliography specifically geared toward student research. A second, annotated bibliography introduces students to all the sources the author consulted when compiling the book. A chronology of important dates gives students an overview, at a glance, of the topic covered. Where applicable, a glossary of terms is included.

In short, the series is designed not only to acquaint readers with the basics of history, but also to make them aware that their lives are a part of an ongoing human saga. Perhaps they will then come to the same realization as famed historian Arnold Toynbee. In his monumental work, *A Study of History*, he wrote about becoming aware of history flowing through him in a mighty current, and of his own life "welling like a wave in the flow of this vast tide."

Piracy in Early Times

Over the years, pirates have been known by many names: buccaneers, freebooters, corsairs, and many others. Regardless of the term used, however, each person who fits the category has done so by engaging in the same activity: theft at sea. At its most basic, piracy requires only two boats and two people: one with some goods, the other with a desire to obtain them and a willingness to use force to do so. Piracy most often occurs on the water, but it is no different morally from burglary, robbery, or any other kind of stealing that takes place on land. As the term is most often used, it also implies that the attacker is not acting in a strictly military capacity: that is, the taking of plunder or the destruction of shipping by a warship is not generally considered piracy.

The odds are good, then, that piracy, in at least some form, dates back to the beginning of human existence. Greed, violence, and an unequal distribution of goods—all are probably as old as human history. Certainly piracy has been in existence for as long as written records have been kept. We know of pirates in the Persian Gulf as early as 5000 B.C.E., for example. The ancient Sumerians and Assyrians had to deal with pirates. So did the early

Egyptians: a document dating from the reign of an early pharaoh discusses the robbery of an Egyptian envoy at sea. The Bible contains references to small-scale pirates who harassed seafarers.

During classical times piracy grew. The fleet belonging to Alexander the Great was attacked by pirates in the Persian Gulf. As the Greek historian Thucydides described piracy in the later stages of the Greek Empire:

> For the Grecians in old time, and of the barbarians both on the continent who lived near the sea, and all who inhabited islands, after they began to cross over more commonly to one another in ships, turned to piracy . . . and falling upon towns that were unfortified, and inhabited like villages, they rifled them, and made most of their livelihood by this means. . . .[1]

By the height of the Roman Empire, piracy had become even more common. Roving bands of buccaneers prowled the Mediterranean, the Atlantic Ocean off the coast of France, and even the English Channel. Their main work was plundering ships carrying goods from one place to another in the extensive Roman trading network, but these pirates, like their later counterparts, did more. They attacked ports and coastal cities. They also carried off people who got in their way, typically holding them for ransom. (Among those who were kidnapped during Roman times was Julius Caesar, later to be dictator.) By any standard, these pirates were quite successful. During the last century of Roman rule, pirates sacked at least four hundred towns along the Mediterranean coastline.

The Mediterranean was a prime territory for piracy. Not only did the Romans raise trade along its shores to a new level, but geographically the sea was nearly perfect for the purposes of buccaneering. Long and narrow, it forced trade ships into certain predictable patterns and routes. Rocky and studded with small islands, it provided excellent cover for pirate crews to lie in wait for prey and to hide from government officials. Moreover, most of the Mediterranean coastline was much better suited to seafaring than to agriculture; this led to a population at home on the sea and without many other ways of making a living. All these factors helped create an atmosphere in which piracy thrived. Similar conditions played roles in most other pirate epidemics through history as well.

AFTER THE CLASSICAL PERIOD

Piracy briefly declined after the end of the Roman Empire, but for the next thousand years and more it would continue to loom large in world history. Buccaneers sailed the coasts of China and Japan, plundered towns and villages in France and England, robbed seafarers on the Mediterranean Sea, and spread terror in many other spots around the world as well. Through the early sixteenth century, the frequency of piracy rose and fell depending on the place and the time. During years of peak pirate activity, the doings in ancient Rome were equaled— or even surpassed.

The best-known pirates of this period were almost certainly the Vikings, Norse seafarers whose raiding expeditions took them throughout much of western Europe and beyond. The Vikings are not always thought of today as pirates. They were an identifiable ethnic group, well

Although their plunder came mostly from coastal towns and villages, most historians classify Vikings as pirates.

within the law where Scandinavian authorities were concerned, whereas most other pirates have been both outlaws and less strictly drawn from one nationality. Their goals and methods, likewise, differed from those of some pirates at other times. The bulk of Viking plunder, for instance, came from coastal towns and villages rather than from other vessels. Nevertheless, pirates can come in many different forms, and most historians class the Vikings among them.

After the Vikings came other European pirates. Some were sponsored by nations, governments, or groups. In 1243, for example, Henry III of England granted a special pirate license to Adam Robernolt and William Le Sauvage, two English sea captains. The licenses charged them "to annoy our enemies at sea and by land wherever they were so able, so that they share with us half of all their gain."[2] Edward I, some years later, offered merchants whose ships had been plundered so-called Commissions of Reprisal, which permitted them to attack any merchant ship they could find that was from the same nation as the ship that had robbed them.

Similar were the pirates sent out to attack the Hanseatic League, which was formed in Germany during the fourteenth century. A loosely connected network of traders and ports in several nations, the Hanseatic League dominated trade throughout northern Europe for many years. Not all principalities in the region joined the league, however, and those that did not were soon left behind economically. As a result, they sent private citizens out in ships to harass the Hanseatic fleet—and to take what plunder they could from them. In response, Hanseatic officials hired private citizens of their own to sail after these pirates; before long, there were pirates battling on both sides.

Of course, some pirates during this period went pirating to serve only themselves. By 1290 the Indian Ocean was infested by entire pirate families—men, women, and children—who sailed in search of booty. As often as not, these families worked together: They sailed in fleets of twenty or more ships, splitting up sections of the ocean between them and making it difficult for any ship to evade their clutches. These pirates were fierce indeed. As one historian writes, some of them "made captured merchants swallow an emetic [a substance that causes vomiting] . . . mixed with sea water so that they would vomit up any concealed pearls and gems."[3] Brutality would be a theme in the development of piracy later on as well.

Piracy of this period also had other dimensions. Long after the Roman era had passed, the Mediterranean Sea was still the home of many buccaneering crews. Through much of the medieval period and into the Renaissance, the dominant group of pirates hailed from North Africa. Known as the Barbary pirates after the Algerian coast they used as their base, these men were Muslims. By the year 1500 they were loosely allied with the Muslim Turkish Empire. While the Barbary pirates were willing to attack Muslim ships on occasion, they turned the full fury of their force on Christian ships that used the Mediterranean. They were quite successful in this religious battle, routinely capturing Italian, Spanish, and French vessels.

Throughout history, pirates have both influenced and been influenced by the world around them.

Most of the pirates of the period before the year 1600 or so are forgotten today, overshadowed by their counterparts from later in history. That is no surprise. Record keeping before 1600 was often poor, and the effects of pirates were usually localized. The pirates of the later seventeenth century were more dramatic figures, better suited for a worldwide stage. It is entirely reasonable that Blackbeard, Bartholomew Roberts, and Thomas Tew should be recalled today and earlier pirates forgotten.

Yet the early pirates helped set the tone for what was to come. The themes of their stories are the same as those of later adventurers. During all eras, piracy has been a very complicated business, driven by forces much more complex than may first appear. Piracy has been conducted for personal gain—and also for political purposes. Men have turned pirate by their own choice—and because the world seemed to offer them no alternatives. Pirates have been motivated by greed, brutality, or national pride. Some pirates have been motivated by all three at once.

All pirates, however, have been the product of the world around them. From the easy availability of plunder to political unrest between nations, pirates have been drawn to their trade at least in part because of conditions they did not control, conditions that were ripe for an outbreak of piracy. But pirates were not only affected by the world in which they lived; they also, in turn, affected life around them. The course of history has been changed in many ways by pirates. Julius Caesar invaded Britain partly in response to the buccaneers who used it as their base, and European history would have been quite different without the influence of the Vikings. As the seventeenth century approached, the pirate impact on history would loom ever larger.

1 Development of the Golden Age

Although piracy was a fact of life throughout classical times and in the Middle Ages, the institution came into its own toward the end of the seventeenth century. This period is often known as piracy's Golden Age. Of course, use of the term *Golden Age* comes from the pirates' point of view: the era cannot be considered a golden age for shippers, naval commanders, or those who lived on any of several coastlines around the world. Indeed, the period was a very difficult one for all those people, because the Golden Age represented perhaps the most concentrated pirate activity in history.

There is much debate about the precise beginning and end of this period. Some historians place its foundations as early as the middle of the sixteenth century. Others argue for a significantly later start. The end of the Golden Age is easier to fix, but even so, there is some disagreement over exact dates. There is little question, though, that the era reached its peak during the years stretching approximately from 1660 to 1720.

While there may be debate over the timing of the Golden Age, there is much less debate over where the Golden Age developed. Nearly all scholars agree that the Caribbean Sea was the cradle of piracy during the time. From the islands of the West Indies—Cuba, Jamaica, and Hispaniola among them—piracy spread outward: first along the Atlantic coastlines and then into the Pacific and Indian Oceans.

The roots of the Golden Age, however, lie significantly before 1660 and in places far from the Caribbean Sea. The forces that resulted in the Golden Age were already under way before the seventeenth century—indeed, before the western European world was aware that Hispaniola and the Caribbean Sea itself even existed. The true beginning of the Golden Age of piracy lies in events and trends that were taking place in Renaissance Europe.

CHANGES IN EUROPEAN SOCIETY

Along with the years just before and after it, the fifteenth century was a time of significant change in Europe. The changes affected all society: not just the political systems of the time, but the cultural, social, and economic structures of European life as well. The events of this period, known as the Renaissance, had enormous impact on the way people thought, acted, and ran their daily lives.

The changes were great. In the cultural realm, a sudden flowering of interest in painting and sculpture sparked a period unmatched in the creation of great works of art. In the political arena, the old European feudal system, which emphasized local control of government, was beginning to die out. Growing in its place was a more modern model of national, centralized authority. Instead of kings ruling at the discretion of the nobles who controlled their private estates, increasingly it was the lords who ruled at the discretion of the kings. And in the scientific realm, thinkers were gradually working their way toward a conception of science that relied on reason, observation, and experimentation rather than on superstition and blind faith.

But perhaps the single most important development of the 1400s was the beginning of exploration on a large scale. Except for the Vikings and perhaps a handful of Irish monks and Basque fishermen, few Europeans had ventured far from the coastline during the medieval period. The Mediterranean Sea was well known, but even the most experienced of medieval seafarers knew only the strip of the Atlantic Ocean

A Renaissance merchant observes the unloading of goods. During this era, people's desire to obtain goods quickly and cheaply led to the beginning of widespread exploration.

Pirates in Jamaica

In the seventeenth century, England took over the former Spanish territory of Jamaica, in part because of the help given them by pirates. A few years later, the Jamaican governing council passed a resolution that explained why piracy might benefit the colony, as quoted in The Age of Piracy *by Robert Carse.*

" . . . 7. It is a great security to the island that the men-of-war [that is, pirates] often intercept Spanish advices and give intelligence to the Governour, which they often did in [earlier official] Colonel D'Oyley's time and since.

8. The said men-of-war bring no small benefit to His Majesty and His Royal Highness by the fifteenths and tenths [the understanding, not always followed, was that a portion of each booty would be given to the king in exchange for permission to loot other ships].

9. They keep many able artificers [craftspeople] at work in Port Royal and elsewhere at Extraordinary wages.

10. Whatsoever they get the soberer part bestow in strengthening their old ships, which in time will grow formidable.

11. They are of great reputation to this island and of terror to the Spaniards and keep up a high military spirit in all the inhabitants.

12. It seems to be the only way to force the Spaniards in time to a free trade, all ways of kindness producing nothing of good neighborhood [that is, being unsuccessful], for though all old commissions have been called in [for privately owned ships to attack Spanish vessels] and no new ones granted, and many of their ships restored, yet they continue all acts of hostility, taking our ships and murdering our people. . . . For which reason it was unanimously concluded that the granting of said commissions did extraordinarily conduce to the strengthening, preservation, enriching, and advancing the settlement of this island."

that hugged the shore. The sea was full of mystery and danger, mariners of the time agreed. Sea monsters lurked; islands sprang up from the ocean floor and stranded ships.

Some areas of the ocean were frozen solid at all times of the year, seafarers believed, and other sections of the seas were doubtless boiling hot.

These notions may seem quaint to us today, but they made a certain amount of sense to people of the early Renaissance. Though sea monsters were not perhaps a legitimate concern, the sea was indeed full of dangers. Ships were dependent on winds and the power of people pulling on oars. There were no engines to carry a vessel safely away from a reef, or to save it from being becalmed for days or even weeks. Ships were small, and their capacity to store food and other supplies was limited; long voyages were difficult, if not impossible.

Navigation, too, was hard. Navigators suffered from an acute lack of information. Charts and maps were not only few but also all too often hopelessly inadequate. Navigational instruments of the time were poor. Sailors had difficulty determining how far north they were, and they had no reliable method of telling how far east or west they had traveled. Even compasses were not what they are today. Under these circumstances, it is not surprising that mariners chose to stay close enough to shore to return easily in case of poor weather and to guide their journeys by familiar landmarks.

Traveling by land, however, was no better. Roads were poor and often nonexistent, and land travelers faced the same supply problems that seafarers did, only worse. Traversing long distances required passing through any number of foreign countries. No one could speak all the possible languages, and hiring interpreters was difficult or impossible. A lucky visitor might be allowed to pass through unmolested, but there was always the chance that the traveler would be officially detained on suspicion of being a spy, an enemy, or simply an infidel. Even those travelers who escaped the wrath of government constantly faced the threat of robbers and highwaymen.

THE AGE OF EXPLORATION

Because of all these concerns, most medieval Europeans rarely left the immediate area of their birth, let alone visited a foreign country. Leaving the continent, in turn, was almost completely unknown. A handful of intrepid travelers had made their way to the far eastern parts of Asia, and others had visited northern Africa and the Middle East. But the average European never visited these places—and most likely never dreamed of visiting them.

In the fifteenth century, however, that began to change. Under the leadership of men such as the Portuguese Prince Henry the Navigator, Europeans began to explore farther and farther afield. Most of these journeys were made by ship. One expedition sailed down the West African coast and past the equator. Another rounded the Cape of Good Hope at the continent's southern tip. Little by little, empty places on maps were filled in. Shipbuilding grew more sophisticated, and navigators similarly became more skilled at their craft. By the beginning of the sixteenth century, European knowledge of the seas extended east to Indonesia and China and west to the Americas.

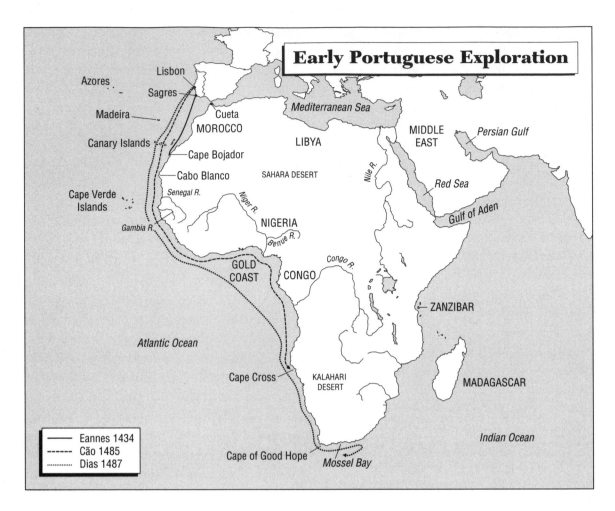

Early Portuguese Exploration

Azores

Lisbon
Sagres

Madeira

Canary Islands

Cape Verde
Islands

Cueta
MOROCCO

Cape Bojador

Cabo Blanco

Senegal R.

Gambia R.

Mediterranean Sea

LIBYA

SAHARA DESERT

Nile R.

Niger R.

NIGERIA

Benue R.

MIDDLE
EAST

Persian Gulf

Red Sea

Gulf of Aden

GOLD
COAST

CONGO

Congo R.

ZANZIBAR

Atlantic Ocean

KALAHARI
DESERT

Cape Cross

MADAGASCAR

Indian Ocean

Cape of Good Hope

Mossel Bay

Eannes 1434
Cão 1485
Dias 1487

These explorations, however, were not made solely for the purpose of gathering knowledge about the world. Nor were they simply for the fun of adventure. Rather, they were made with political and economic goals in mind. The single most important reason behind all this adventuring was to find a direct and easy path to eastern Asia and its store of spices, silks, and other valuable materials. These items were much desired in Europe, but because of the distance involved had to be transported through land routes across Asia, usually by a series of trades that brought the materials ever closer to Europe. That system drove up the price of the goods. It also put Europeans at the mercy of the traders, who could cut off the supply if they chose for any reason whatsoever. The voyages around Africa—and, for that matter, the first voyages to America—were made with the goal of reaching the East Indies.

But much of what the explorers found in the New World proved to be of even greater value to Europeans than spices, cloth, or a new trade route. Notable among these were precious metals: gold, silver, and others much more common in parts of the New World than in Europe itself. But this list included plants and foods as well, especially sugar, chocolate, and tobacco. It also included the human cargo of slaves, taken from Africa and shipped to the New World to work on plantations.

Europeans quickly did whatever they needed to do to locate the valuables and to make use of them. Early in the sixteenth century the Spanish explorer and soldier Hernán Cortés destroyed the Aztec Empire in central Mexico in his search for jewels and gold, and Cortés's

countryman Francisco Pizarro did the same to the Inca of Peru. The transatlantic slave trade itself began only a few years after Columbus's initial American voyage. Where Europeans could, they took what they wanted; where they lacked sufficient force, they bartered. Before long, ships laden with their prizes began to cross the oceans, destined for the royal treasury or for the pockets of those wealthy investors who backed private voyages.

POLITICAL CONSIDERATIONS

However, the booty was not divided evenly among all seafaring nations. Spain and Portugal were the early leaders in exploration and mighty military powers as well, and they laid the first and strongest claims to the lands they found. Spain took Mexico, Central America, and most of the Caribbean. The Spanish would have taken all of South America as well, but Portugal complained and the pope stepped in. Two compromises were worked out, and by 1494 Portugal had control of Brazil, while Spain was assigned the rest of the continent. The territorial claims led to monopolies on the goods those territories contained: Ships from other nations were typically not permitted to enter Spanish or Portuguese waters, even for trading purposes.

The dominance of Spain and Portugal, however, did not sit well with other nations. France, England, and the Netherlands, in particular, objected to their inability to obtain territories outside of Europe. Without territories, they could not hope to gain an edge in trade and benefit from the new-found wealth. Spain and Portugal—particularly Spain, the single most dominant nation in Europe at the time—would continue to grow in economic and political power, and the other nations would be left out. "The strength of the Spaniards doth grow altogether from the mines of her treasure,"[4] observed an Englishman in 1585, and many agreed with him.

Throughout the sixteenth century, England, France, and the Netherlands did their best to reduce Spain's power and gain their own foothold in the Americas. To be sure, there were reasons for conflict besides trade and territorial concerns: By the end of the 1500s, Spain was a staunchly Catholic nation, while England and the Netherlands had installed Protestant-leaning governments. However, the trade issue was uppermost in the minds of Spain's enemies. Hostilities, declared and undeclared, carried the day during most of the century. On the surface, these hostilities favored Spain. After all, Spain had the best ships, the best captains, and the most money. Taking on the full strength of the Spanish navy seemed a dangerous and foolhardy task.

Spain, however, did have a noticeable weakness. The Spanish Empire was enormous—so vast that it could not be properly patrolled by Spanish ships. A small, fast ship from England or the Netherlands could easily enter Spanish territory without any Spanish officials knowing. Once inside, the sailors could and did set up trading depots and even small colonies. The Caribbean was full of out-of-the-way islands and unknown anchorages. By 1527 the English were already sneaking ships into Spanish waters this way, and by the

Pirates took advantage of hidden coves on small islands to attack treasure-laden Spanish vessels.

1560s the problem was bad enough for the Spanish government to strongly remind its colonists in the West Indies that "no English vessel should be allowed under any pretext to trade there."[5]

Better still for Spain's enemies, it turned out that these small ships and out-of-the-way islands were ideal for launching attacks against Spain. A fast ship could rise up from seemingly nowhere, attack a ponderous treasure-laden ship or a small trad-ing port, and make off with valuables long before an alarm could be raised. Known as privateers, these captains took full advantage for their country of Spain's inability to police its possessions.

Little by little throughout the second half of the 1500s, these ships harassed Spanish fleets and interfered with Spanish domin-ion of the area. They did their work well. By the beginning of the seventeenth cen-tury, Spain was no longer as powerful as it had been. Before the middle of the century, its enemies had even established entire colonies in what had been Spanish territory. The French took Martinique and half of the island of Hispaniola. The Dutch, meanwhile, took Tobago, Curaçao, and many other smaller islands, and the English found a foothold in Barbados and Jamaica, among others.

Part of Spain's decline was attributable to the defeat of the mighty Spanish Armada, or fleet of warships, off the coast of England in 1588. Defeating the Armada represented a massive and completely unexpected victory for the English that catapulted them into the highest ranks of naval powers. But just as important was the gradual wearing down of Spain's resources in losing millions of dollars' worth of valuable merchandise to Dutch, English, and French ships year after year.

THE GOLDEN AGE

This was the background, then, for the Golden Age of piracy. The struggle for trade supremacy in the New World—and similar developments in Asia—led indirectly to the brutal crews of pirates who ruled the seas during the 1600s. So, too, did the development of better navigational instruments and the faster ships that were a product of the Age of Exploration. From sociology to politics and from economics to technology, the events of the years leading up to the Golden Age made the careers of such pirates as Bartholomew Roberts, Blackbeard, and William Kidd almost inevitable. Indeed, at the beginning of the seventeenth century,

conditions in the Caribbean were ripe for the flourishing of piracy as had never happened before—and has never occurred since.

Most obvious, perhaps, was the issue of plunder. Piracy only makes sense if there is a prospect of a reasonable payoff: that is, if the goods carried on a ship are likely to be valuable enough to support those who raid it. Ships had not always carried cargo valuable enough to make stealing pay. In earlier times, even experienced seamen who did not mind breaking the law often chose not to engage in piracy, simply because very few could capture enough plunder from passing ships to make it worth their while.

That all changed dramatically at the beginning of the Golden Age. Dizzying amounts of booty were sailing past the islands of the Caribbean nearly every day, it seemed. A few well-chosen prizes could allow a pirate to settle down in wealth and peace—a far cry from the relatively poor payoffs of earlier years. The sheer value of the available treasure drew pirates to the Caribbean—and sparked many others to turn pirate. "Within the space of two years the riches of the country were much increased," wrote an observer about conditions on one of the sea's many islets. "The number of Pirates did augment so fast [that] there were to be numbered in that small island and port above twenty ships of this sort of people."[6]

The wars that had affected the Caribbean were another reason for the beginning of the Golden Age. The constant struggles between Spain and its enemies established an atmosphere of lawlessness in the West Indies. Islands that technically belonged to Spain were nevertheless settled by the Dutch, the French, or the English. Ships attacked one another with little or no provocation; whole populations retreated inland to avoid the fighting. Raids in the name of one country or another were constant. Might made right; indeed, force was all that really mattered. The pirates of the Golden Age learned their lessons well. Their own countries had already showed them the way toward violence. As one historian puts it, "When adventurous spirits have been [hired] to sail the seas and plunder the ships of another nation, it is but a step forward to continue that fine work without a commission after the war is over."[7]

The wars played another important role as well. Spain had already showed itself unable to patrol the West Indies successfully. Especially after the defeat of the Armada, the Spanish did not have nearly the number of warships they would require to do so—and many of the ones they did have were needed in Europe. It was clear to would-be pirates that the Spanish

The crew of a ship watches helplessly as pirates help themselves to a fortune in treasure.

After the defeat of the Spanish Armada, Spain did not have enough ships to protect its possessions around the world.

would have a difficult time defending against piracy, which lessened the risk of attacking.

As for the other European powers, they were neither ready to act as police officer nor interested in doing so. Indeed, at first these powers perceived the pirates as acting in their own best interest. An enemy of the Spanish, they reasoned, was a friend of theirs. "The French and English Governors in the West Indies," sums up one writer, "either openly, or by connivance, gave constant encouragement to the Buccaneers."[8] The Golden Age would be well under way before the English and the French decided that piracy was a hindrance rather than a help.

A NEW FRONTIER

A third related reason for the Golden Age involved the Caribbean's status as a frontier. During the Golden Age whole colonies of drifters, dreamers, and adventurers sprang up. Some of these people were criminals. Others were servants, naval sailors, or even gentlemen who had opted for another career. Like settlers to any frontier since history began, these men were drawn to the Caribbean in search of wealth, excitement, and a chance to start over where no one knew them.

Life in the islands was not especially dramatic or easy, however. For the most part, these drifters stayed away from the most settled areas, inhabiting small islands and the least desirable sections of the larger ones. They ate cows, goats, and pigs introduced to the islands by earlier Europeans, and cooked the meat on an open grill. (This habit gave them the name of *boucanier*, a French term meaning one who cooks his food barbecue-style; this in turn gave rise to our word *buccaneer*.) They eked out a meager living trading dried meat with nearby settlers and with sea captains.

PETER THE GREAT

Perhaps the first major pirate raid of the Golden Age was carried out by Peter the Great, or Pierre le Grand, who attacked a Spanish admiral's ship. This raid was described by Alexander Exquemelin in his book The Buccaneers of America.

"The Boat wherein Pierre le Grand was with his companions, had now been at sea a long time, without finding anything . . . suitable to make a prey. And now their provisions beginning to fail, they could keep themselves no longer upon the ocean, or they must of necessity starve. Being almost reduced to despair, they espied a great ship belonging to the Spanish flota [fleet], which had separated from the rest. This bulky vessel they resolved to set upon and take, or die in the attempt. Hereupon they made sail towards her, with design to view her strength. And although they judged this vessel to be far above their forces, yet the covetousness of such a prey, and the extremity of fortune they were reduced to, made them adventure on such an enterprise. . . . It was in the dusk of the evening, or soon after, when this great action was performed. But before it was begun, they gave orders to the surgeon of the boat to bore a hole in the sides thereof, to the intent that, their own vessel sinking under them, they might be compelled to attack more vigorously, and endeavour more hastily to run aboard the great ship. This was performed accordingly; and without any other arms than a pistol in one of their hands and a sword in the other, they immediately climbed up the sides of the ship, and ran altogether [all together] into the great cabin, where they found the Captain, with several of his companions, playing at cards. Here they set a pistol to his breast, commanding him to deliver up the ship to their obedience. The Spaniards seeing the Pirates aboard their ship, without scarce having seen them at sea, cried out, 'Jesus bless us! Are these devils, or what are they?'"

It soon became clear, however, that piracy was a better option, providing both a higher standard of living and a more exciting way of life. "Those that were poore and had nothing but from hand to mouth," explained an observer, "turned Pirats."[9] Here the geography of the West Indies played a significant role in beginning the Golden Age. By some accounts, the first pirate expeditions of the period were raised among a community of drifters who had taken over the island of La Tortuga. La Tortuga is located on a narrow sea passage that runs between two major islands, Cuba and Hispaniola. Ships typically chose to go through the passage rather than adding miles to their voyage by navigating around one of the big islands.

The steady stream of treasure inspired the La Tortuga buccaneers to take to the sea, and the hideouts and lairs available to them provided ample opportunity to take the merchant fleet by surprise. According to one popular story, an early La Tortuga pirate known as Peter the Great staged a night raid on a Spanish vessel. The pirates were so silent and had hidden themselves so well that the Spanish captain was unaware of them until they boarded his ship. "The ship is invaded by devils,"[10] the captain is supposed to have cried, half suspecting that the invaders had come out of nowhere.

The plunder taken by these early pirates made many of them wealthy men indeed. "I could name a number of men who came out [to the Caribbean] as indentured servants," wrote a French priest of the time, "who are now such great seigneurs [lords] that they cannot walk a step but must now always ride in their carriages and six horses."[11] The richer they grew, the more powerful they became as well, and their success encouraged others to join the piratical trade.

WIDENING OF PIRATE TERRITORY

Although piracy's Golden Age had begun in the Caribbean Sea, it did not remain restricted to that part of the globe for long. From the West Indies, pirate bands soon began to spread outward. Coastal populations in Panama and the South American mainland soon became targets. Gradually pirates moved into the Pacific and north to the coastline of what is now the United States. "North and South America are infested with these rogues,"[12] complained the governor of Bermuda in 1717.

The main reason for the outward movement was a gradual diminishing of shipping throughout the Caribbean. For this, the pirates had only themselves to blame. Increasingly, Spain did not dare to send ships into the Caribbean at all. Neither did other nations. There were simply too many pirates, and the pirates were too well armed and too powerful. As the Golden Age wore on and pirates became more bold and more brutal, shipping ground nearly to a halt. Merchants of all nationalities asked themselves why they should bother sending ships through the West Indies if they were only going to be captured by the likes of Bartholomew Roberts and his men, and most had no good answers.

Partly as a result of the Caribbean pirates, too, shipping had become a worldwide proposition. Spain increasingly turned its attention to the Pacific. Ships carrying spices, cloth, and precious metals plied back and forth from Europe to Peru, the Philippines, and other destinations just as they had once sailed between Spain and the Caribbean. India sent ships through the Indian Ocean and into the Pacific. Other nations did the same. Wherever these heavily laden ships sailed, the pirates followed. "Whole [pirate] companies both from England and our American colonies flocked thither," wrote a 1701 pamphleteer about a section of the ocean off eastern Asia.[13]

This, too, represented a change from earlier pirates. Pirates of previous eras had been active in only a small stretch of ocean—the Mediterranean Sea, perhaps, or the few dozen miles off Europe's western coastline.

With a few exceptions, notably the Vikings, these early pirates had basically waited for ships to come to them. In contrast, pirates of the Golden Age swept across virtually the entire world. Technology of navigation and shipbuilding now allowed it, and the worldwide nature of shipping required it. Driven by what one pirate called "the sacred hunger of gold,"[14] buccaneers were happy to track their prey down wherever that might take them. Thus, from Madagascar to Peru and from Indonesia to Virginia, the buccaneers ruled the oceans. A pirate crew could be in Africa one summer and off the coast of South America the next, attacking spice ships near India and coastal settlements of Central America with equal abandon.

The pirates certainly logged many thousands of miles. "On first coming out, they

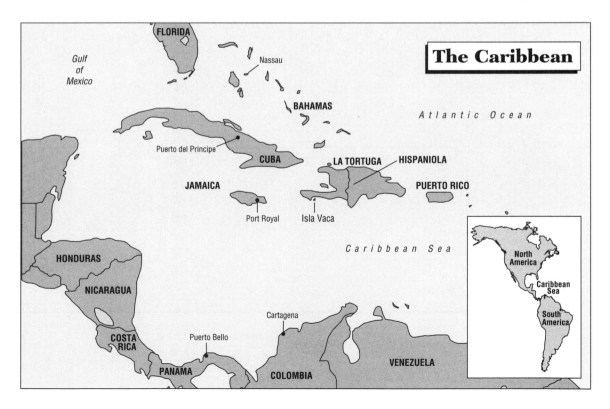

generally go first to the Isle of May for salt," wrote an observer, describing a typical pirate journey of the late seventeenth century, "then to Fernando for water, then round the Cape of Good Hope to Madagascar to victual [take on food] and water." From there they sailed to the northern Indian Ocean to wait for merchants "who must come at a certain time [of year] because of the trade wind."[15] The round trip between the Caribbean and the East Indies could take a year and involve a journey of some twenty thousand miles—but was well worth the possible riches that awaited a clever and courageous crew.

The Golden Age for pirates had arrived. Pirates had become the scourges of the entire world. The Golden Age was an era when pirates roamed with little fear of reprisal; an era when crime truly did pay; an era in which a few adventuresome and morally questionable men could borrow or steal a ship and become rich overnight. The Golden Age did not last long, but it certainly made its mark on history.

2 Lives of the Pirates

Today, years after the Golden Age, the life of a pirate strikes many people as romantic. The pirate's life is viewed as one of perpetual drama, adventure, and excitement—appealing in comparison to the scheduled, organized, relatively uneventful lives led by many Americans today. Popular culture has scrubbed the rough edges off pirates and made them seem almost heroic. Pirates are often seen as brave men, clever and resourceful, succeeding against overwhelming odds. Stories of famous pirates and pictures of pirates in action usually focus on certain themes and images that tend to fire up the imagination. The drama of sword fights, the finery of pirate captains, the excitement of a skull-and-crossbones flag rippling in the sea breeze, the intrigue of buried treasure . . . this is the stuff of which legends are made.

The reality of pirate life, however, was quite different from the romanticized view many Americans have of it today. Pirates were real people, not simply fictional creations. Real people bleed and die during sword fights; real people suffer from lack of food and water when times grow hard, as they often did for pirates. English philosopher Thomas Hobbes once described an uncivilized state of nature as full of "continual fear and danger of violent death"; life in such a state, he went on, was "nasty, brutish, and short."[16] Hobbes could easily have been describing a pirate's life. For the most part, pirates did not live long, and their lives were often bitterly harsh. For every romantic moment of glory aboard a pirate ship, there were many, many more moments of terror, misery, and wanton violence.

CAPTAINS

One widespread belief about piracy is that the pirate captain held complete control over his crew. From Captain Kidd to the fearsome Blackbeard, every captain supposedly ruled his company with a metaphoric iron fist—making all the decisions and meting out punishment to those luckless members of the crew who crossed him. In reality, however, this control was mainly a myth. The surprising truth is that pirate captains rarely had much more authority than the lowliest common sailor. By the time of the Golden Age, the pirate ship was perhaps the most democratic place on earth.

The captain was certainly an important person on board ship. He was the acknowledged leader, charged with determining

Even well-known captains like Captain Kidd (pictured) held very little power when the ship was not engaged in battle.

the course of the ship and given several other responsibilities as well. When the pirates were busy attacking a merchant ship, his role was particularly large. Once the battle began, the captain's was the only voice that mattered. He gave the signal to start the attack and ordered his men where he saw fit. Those who disobeyed came to regret it: "The captain's power is uncontrollable in chase or in battle," wrote one observer, "drubbing [beating], cutting [with a sword or knife], or even shooting anyone who does deny his command."[17]

Other than in battle, however, the captain did not enjoy much power beyond that held by regular crew members. His position was not at all the same as his counterpart on board a merchant ship or a naval vessel. Those captains were the sole leaders of their ships; the pirate captain, in contrast, was merely one among equals. According to pirate tradition, for example, a captain could not issue a single order to a crewman as long as no fighting was taking place. Likewise, though the captain was entitled to a larger share of the loot than the rest of the crew, the difference was small. A pirate named Alexander Esquemeling, or Exquemelin, reported in 1684 that the captain "was allotted five or six portions to what the ordinary seamen have,"[18] but other sources place the number much lower—three times the usual ration, double it, or perhaps even less.

The pirate captain also had few outward symbols of his office. To be sure, he had his own cabin on board the ship, and he often had finer clothes than any member of the crew. Similarly, he was often entitled to better and fancier food, dishes, and cutlery. However, none of these things was truly his. "Every man may at his pleasure intrude into the captain's cabin," reported a writer of the seventeenth century, "swear at him, or take what part of his victuals or drink that may please them without his offering to deny them."[19] Even the most feared pirate captains had to play by the rules.

Indeed, a wise captain made sure to treat the crew as he would like to be treated. Doing so was not only fair and ethical but was also in his own best interest. Except in a few cases, the captain of a pirate ship was typically elected by majority vote of the crew—and could be deposed in favor of someone else at almost any time if the crew disagreed with his decisions. "They only permit him to be captain on condition that they may be captain over him,"[20] wrote an observer. This system often led to extremely rapid changes of captain. According to a writer of the time, one ship went through thirteen different captains in the space of less than a year. Others surely approached this record.

Reasons for deposing a captain were many. Excessive use of force against crew members was one, as was letting the position inflate his sense of self-importance. Captains who began telling crewmen what to do outside of battle were promptly dismissed. As a member of Bartholomew Roberts's crew put it:

> Should a Captain be so sawcy as to exceed Prescription at any time, why down with Him; it will be a Caution [warning] after he is dead, to his successors, of what a fatal Consequence any sort of assuming may be. . . . [I]t is my advice, that, while we are sober, we pitch upon a Man of Courage, and skill'd in Navigation, one, who by his Council and Bravery seems best able to defend this Commonwealth, and ward us from Dangers and Tempests of an instable Element, and the fatal Consequences of Anarchy.[21]

Indeed, incompetence was probably the single leading cause of changed captains. Some were far from "skill'd in Navigation": Walter Kennedy, aiming for Ireland, ran aground in a Scottish creek instead. More common were those who were too fearful in planning attacks and those who were too rash. In either case, crewmen soon grew disgusted with the lack of income and rebelled accordingly.

However, a captain who was skilled at winning booty could keep a command for months, occasionally years. England's Henry Morgan, for example, served as captain of one band of pirates more or less continuously between 1668 and 1672. But the lifespan of a pirate was notoriously short, and few well-known captains survived long enough to achieve such a record. Even the legendary Blackbeard, also known as Edward Teach, commanded his ship, the *Queen Anne's Revenge*, for less than two years before being killed in a fight with a naval lieutenant.

Because of the dangers involved in piracy, even fearsome pirates like Blackbeard (pictured, slain) rarely commanded vessels for more than a few months.

Quartermasters

Next in rank to the captain—and in some ways ranking above him—was the quartermaster. "The captain can do nothing which the quartermaster does not approve of," observed Daniel Defoe, who in addition to being the author of *Robinson Crusoe* wrote one of the most famous books on pirates. The quartermaster held an important position of trust: "The quartermaster," Defoe continued, "is an humble imitation of the Roman tribune, for he speaks for and looks after the interest of the company."[22] Like the captain, the quartermaster was typically elected by the crew, but he was more likely to remain in power over time.

The quartermaster's duties were many. He was in charge of dealing out the booty after each successful attack. In order to ensure fairness and lack of complaints, it was important to elect someone to the office who commanded respect. Likewise, he helped the captain with navigation, so he needed to be a skilled seaman. The quartermaster also required courage, as he generally was the leader of any group of pirates that actually boarded a merchant ship.

The quartermaster had another important role as well. The captain could not order disciplinary measures against crew members who broke rules, even relatively minor ones. That job was left, instead, to the quartermaster. The quartermaster tried to work out compromises between men who quarreled on board the ship; when that failed, he determined punishment for these and other offenses. In the case of a quarrel, this often meant taking the two participants to an out-of-the-way location such as a small island, where they would fight until one was injured—or sometimes dead. Organizing and umpiring this form of a duel was the quartermaster's job.

The typical pirate crew included a number of other officers as well. Many of these positions, however, were held only when there were enough pirates to justify having them. Others were elegant titles attached to few responsibilities and fewer privileges. Pirate lieutenants, for example, served as a kind of vice captain: they were expected to take over if a captain was killed in the middle of a fight, but other than that had nothing particular to do.

To be sure, some jobs were critical. Every ship needed a capable navigator to help the captain plot courses and determine the correct direction around hazards. So-called "sailing masters" carried out this task on most pirate ships. Boatswains, or bos'uns, took care of the sails and the supplies while also being responsible for the maintenance of the ship. Skilled artisans, from carpenters on up to surgeons, were also an essential part of any voyage.

Common Sailors

But despite the influence of the captain, the quartermaster, and even the surgeon, the pirate crew itself was fundamentally in charge of the ship. Men who joined the crew were entitled to certain rights and privileges, many more than what they would enjoy as a merchantman or in the navy of any sea power. "Every man shall have an equal vote in affairs of the moment," began the list of articles, or rules, signed by every one of Bartholomew Roberts's crew members. "He

EDWARD LOW'S ARTICLES

"1. The Captain is to have two full Shares; the [quarter] Master is to have one Share and one Half; The Doctor, Mate, Gunner and Boatswain, one Share and one Quarter.

2. He that shall be found guilty of taking up any Unlawfull Weapon on Board the Privateer or any other prize by us taken, so as to Strike or Abuse one another in any regard, shall suffer what Punishment the Captain and Majority of the Company shall see fit.

3. He that shall be found Guilty of Cowardice in the time of Ingagements, shall suffer what Punishment the Captain and Majority of the Company shall think fit.

4. If any Gold, Jewels, Silver, &c. be found on Board of any Prize or Prizes to the value of a Piece of Eight, & the finder do not deliver it to the Quarter Master in the space of 24 hours he shall suffer what Punishment the Captain and Majority of the Company shall think fit.

5. He that is found Guilty of Gaming, or Defrauding one another to the Value of a Ryal of Plate [a small coin], shall suffer what Punishment the Captain and Majority of the Company shall think fit.

6. He that shall have the Misfortune to loose a Limb in time of Engagement, shall have the Sum of Six hundred pieces of Eight, and remain aboard as long as he shall think fit.

7. Good Quarters to be given when Craved.

8. He that sees a Sail first, shall have the best Pistol or Small Arm aboard of her.

9. He that shall be guilty of Drunkenness in time of Engagement shall suffer what Punishment the Captain and Majority of the Company shall think fit.

10. No Snaping [setting off] of Guns in the Hould."

shall have an equal title to the fresh provisions or strong liquors at any time seized, and shall use them at pleasure unless a scarcity may make it necessary for the common good that a retrenchment [cutting back] may be voted."[23]

PENALTIES

If a pirate was tried and found guilty, he was often given the death penalty. The 1700 trial of John Houghling in Virginia ended in conviction. These instructions to the sheriff of Princess Anne County, where Houghling's execution was to take place, are quoted by Lloyd Haynes Williams in Pirates of Colonial Virginia.

"Whereas John Hoogling Marriner at a session of Oyer and Terminer [a court proceeding] held at Elizabeth City Court house the 14th day of this Instant [month] May, hath been arraigned and convicted of a Pyracy and Robbery committed upon the high seas and within the Jurisdiction of the Admiralty of England on the Shipp Pensilvania Merchant for which he hath received sentence of death.

These are therefore in his Majesties Name to require you forthwith to receive the said John Hoogling into your custody from the Sheriff of Elizabeth City County and him to keep in safe custody. And on Friday the 24th day of this Instant May You are to cause the said John Hoogling to be carried to the place of Execution and between the houres of Eleven and One of the same day to hang the said John Hoogling upon a Gibbett to be erected by you for that purpose up by the Neck till he be dead, dead, dead and there to let him remaine and hang[;] for so doing[,] this shall be your warrant[,] of which you are to make due Returne to his Majesties Secretarys Office at James City. . . ."

These and similar articles were law aboard pirate ships. They guaranteed each man a fair share of whatever treasure might be obtained. The share was usually specified in advance, and the quartermaster was thus bound to observe the rule in doling out the wealth. They also provided an early sort of workers' compensation system in which the injured were entitled to extra benefits. "If any man should Loose a Joynt in ye said service," read one such clause in a ship's articles, "he should have a hundred pieces of 8 [Spanish silver coins, so named because they were worth one-eighth of a Spanish real, the basic unit of currency]."[24] The loss of a full limb, an eye, or the ability to walk entitled a pirate to even more, and by most accounts these extra payments were rigidly observed.

Indeed, the crew did hold power. Not only could they choose their captains and other officers, but they were also the only ones able to inflict serious punishment on one another. In cases of significant crimes

PIRATES

and matters of carelessness, a jury would be formed from among the pirates and a suitable punishment determined. For matters such as hitting another crewman or walking around the powder room while smoking a pipe—an act that could result in an explosion—the usual penalty was Moses' Law: a flogging consisting of thirty-nine lashes from a length of tarred rope held by the quartermaster.

Being flogged was bad enough. A beating, especially one that continued as long as Moses' Law required, could leave scars or even knock a pirate unconscious. However, the punishment for some crimes could sometimes be much, much worse. This was especially true when it came to matters that damaged group unity among the sailors. The murder of one sailor by another was an obvious example, but it was far from the only one. Nearly all rules of conduct, for instance, forbade theft among crew members. Theft, whether of personal items or of shares of loot, was especially bad for morale: It led to suspicion and to a lack of trust, dangerous in a business where all had to rely on one another for success—and, for that matter, for life. The articles signed by John Phillips's crew in 1723 took even relatively minor thefts seriously: "to the Value of a Piece of Eight," Phillips's rules specified.[25]

Likewise, desertion from the crew was dealt with swiftly and brutally. This policy made sense, too. A deserter might be tempted to take secrets with him, might even be persuaded to tell the authorities what he knew about the captain's methods and hideouts. Moreover, a man who deserted during a battle was declaring his own life more valuable than those of his comrades. Concern over desertion was widespread; many crews forbade any pirate to leave the ship before the end of the voyage for any reason whatsoever. Once aboard a pirate ship, a crewman had to expect to stay there until the group agreed to go their separate ways, or the journey ended in disaster. The only exception might be a crew member of long standing who had earned the trust of others and who could be counted upon not to turn traitor, and even he had to ask permission. Otherwise, those who left the ship and were caught were rarely given second chances.

The punishments for murder, theft, and desertion were uncommonly vicious. If a pirate was lucky, he would simply be shot. If he was unlucky, he would be subject to any of several extremely unpleasant tortures leading ultimately to death. Murder, for example, might be punished by tying the murderer to his victim's corpse and dropping the package into the sea, with drowning the inevitable result. A similar penalty, known as "keelhauling," involved tying an offender up and pulling him slowly underneath the keel of the ship. Most drowned. Those who did not usually died anyway, from wounds received by being scraped against the barnacle-encrusted hull.

More common was what pirates called "marooning." A pirate sentenced to this fate was abandoned on a small deserted island, often one so tiny it would be covered by water at high tide. Even a larger island rarely contained much in the way of food, shelter, or fresh water. If the crew was feeling merciful, they would give the criminal a gun and a few bullets, to be used for suicide when heat, hunger, and thirst became too great. If not, then the poor pirate could only sit and wait for the end.

In some cases, too, marooned pirates were injured before being dropped ashore. "If any man rob another," warned Roberts's articles, "he shall have his nose and ears slit, and be put ashore where he shall be sure to encounter hardships."[26] Not all men who were marooned died as a result. Some managed to find their way to safety; others were rescued by their fellow crewmen after they had changed their minds. But for most, marooning was an irreversible penalty.

WORK, BOREDOM, AND AMUSEMENTS

Pirates spent only a small portion of their time actually looting, plundering, and engaged in battle. By far the largest percentage of their hours were spent cruising the seas in search of prey, making necessary repairs to the ship, or hiding out from sea patrols. This aspect of pirate life was far from glorious and far from dramatic. Indeed, most of pirate life consisted of hard work and boredom—a volatile combination that may well have made some pirates long for the excitement of a sea battle.

Marooning was a common punishment for many offenses. Without food, water, or shelter, marooned pirates were destined to perish.

Hard work was of particular importance aboard a pirate ship. Running a ship—any ship at all—required strength and endurance. In bad weather, crews worked themselves into exhaustion trying to keep their sails intact and their ship from capsizing. Even in good weather, sails had to be raised and lowered, and supplies had to be brought up from the hold.

Maintenance was essential, too. Sailors spent enormous amounts of time on routine tasks like coiling and splicing rope and scrubbing down the decks. Pirate crews fought a usually losing battle against rot and decay and the ravages of the sea. Even in the best of times their ships leaked. Crews were constantly patching holes and bailing water that collected in the bottom of the ship. Sails ripped apart, too, and had to be fixed or replaced. Broken masts or tillers were worse; they could send a ship careening into a rock or out of control, so they had to be checked carefully as often as possible and replaced or repaired at the earliest sign of distress.

Nature had its say as well. A parasite called the teredo worm, common in the tropics, attached itself to the hulls of pirate ships and tunneled through the wood like a termite. Left alone, the worms would slow down the ship and eventually sink it. To avoid this fate, pirates had to clean the bottom of the ship about three times a year. Cleaning required careening the ship: beaching it, using ropes to turn it partway onto its side, and then coating it with a mixture of tar and other substances to reinforce the wood and keep the worms at bay. This was backbreaking labor; it was dangerous, too, for the ship was useless while being careened and the pirates were left open to easy attack.

The flip side of hard work was boredom. Hours of routine and unexciting labor one day led seamlessly into the next. Thus, diversions were essential. Gambling was one especially favored pastime. Pirates were enthusiastic gamblers, ready to bet on all sorts of games involving dice and cards. These games were ideal for long crossings of empty ocean; they required little space, less equipment, and a healthy desire to increase one's wealth. Canny pirates doubled or tripled their shares of booty in a few days, while less skilled and unlucky players were apt to lose much of theirs. Of course, not all wins were accomplished strictly through honesty. "For a gamester that would win without hazarding much his money," a pirate-era gambling handbook instructed would-be cheaters, "dice that will run very seldom otherwise but Sixes, Cinques [fives], Quarters [fours], &c., are very necessary."[27]

Another common amusement was drinking. Rum, brandy, wine, and all other kinds of alcoholic beverages were exceedingly popular among the buccaneers. "Good Liquor to Sailors is preferable to Clothing,"[28] wrote one pirate observer, and most pirates certainly agreed. Many drank to excess during their spare time, opening one cask of liquor after another until many members of the crew were entirely drunk. A handful of pirate captains banned liquor altogether, believing that consumption would interfere with the crew's judgment during battle and might promote disunity among the men. Others limited the times and places when men could drink, hoping to forestall the

Often captured from merchant vessels, musicians on board a pirate ship provided music and entertainment for the crew.

worst kinds of drunkenness. "If any of the crew desire to drink after [eight at night]," commanded Bartholomew Roberts's rules, "they shall sit upon the open deck without lights."[29]

Pirates also enjoyed the drama of mock trials. One pirate would be chosen to defend himself against an imaginary charge. Other crewmen took on the roles of judge, lawyers, jurors, and other such courtroom personnel. Daniel Defoe reported on one trial that took place in 1721. "Here is a fellow before you that is a sad dog, a sad sad dog," Defoe quoted the prosecutor as saying, "and I humbly hope your Lordship [that is, the judge] will order him to be hanged out of the way immediately."[30] The trial ended, as most did, with a "death"

sentence—never carried out, although one young "defendant," fearing the court was in earnest, chopped off the prosecutor's arm in self-defense. These games helped pirates face the reality that they were outlaws and could be executed if they were ever captured.

And a few pirates whiled away their leisure hours with music and books, especially the Bible. Many of the most successful pirate ships carried musicians, a so-called pirate orchestra usually made up of seamen captured from merchant ships. These men played music so the pirates could dance and sing, typically dances and songs that were popular either among merchant ship crews or in nearby ports. The orchestra members often knew little or nothing about

MARY READ

Mary Read was one of two female pirates known to have sailed during the Golden Age, though there may well have been others. When a young woman, Read disguised herself as a man and joined an army regiment in the Netherlands, as quoted in Pirates, Highwaymen, and Adventurers *by Eric Partridge.*

"Soon tiring of this, she deserted, and shipped herself aboard a vessel bound for the West Indies. The ship was taken by an English pirate, Captain Rackam, and Mary joined his crew as a seaman.

She was at New Providence Island, Bahama, when [governor] Woodes Rogers came there with a royal pardon to all pirates, and she shipped herself aboard a privateer sent out by Rogers to cruise against the Spaniards. The crew mutinied and again became pirates.

She now sailed under Captain Rackam, who had with him another woman pirate, Anne Bonny. They took a large number of ships belonging to Jamaica, and out of one of these took prisoner 'a young fellow of engaging behaviour' with whom Mary fell deeply in love. This young fellow had a quarrel with one of the pirates, and as the ship lay at anchor they were to go fight it out on shore according to pirate law. Mary, to save her lover, picked a quarrel with the same pirate, and managed to have her duel at once, and fighting with sword and pistol killed him on the spot.

She now married the young man 'of engaging behaviour,' and not long after was taken prisoner with Captain Rackam and the rest of the crew to Jamaica. She was tried at St. Jago de la Vega in Jamaica, and on November 28th, 1720, was convicted, but died in prison soon after of a violent fever."

Disguising herself as a man, Mary Read joined a pirate crew and sailed on many adventures.

music, and their instruments were far from new. Then again, the pirates turned this lack into a virtue. Pirate orchestras played during attacks, and the cacophony created by the crashing of drums and wailing of oboes helped intimidate the merchant crews.

LIVING CONDITIONS

Unfortunately, all the amusements in the world could not make up for the conditions in which the pirates lived. Ships of the Golden Age were far from comfortable, and pirate ships were worse than most. Small and cramped to begin with, most pirate ships were loaded with extra crewmen—many more than the same ship would have carried as a merchant ship—and so quarters were extremely tight. Most of the men slept in the forecastle, or fo'c's'le, below decks at the front of the ship, but even with staggered sleeping shifts, the space was not at all suitable for so many.

Worse, leaks, storms, and the lack of fresh air below decks meant that the space soon grew wet, stale, and smelly. The combination was a perfect incubator for the spread of disease. Men suffered from all manner of illnesses brought on or made worse by the squalid conditions. Colds, pneumonia, and other respiratory diseases made the rounds, and sicknesses such as typhoid, dysentery, and influenza spread quickly in the hot, wet, close quarters given to the men. Bugs and rats infested the holds and the living areas, making the problem worse. Sometimes crews tried to rid the ship of disease by burning pots of tar below the decks, but the resulting smoke did little

to clean things up and nothing to eradicate diseases already established on board the ship. There was virtually no escape: the men were packed in tightly, and their frequent travels brought them into contact with diseases against which they had no natural immunities. On some ships, half or more of the original crew died of disease.

The situation was exacerbated by hard work and poor nutrition. Of the two, poor nutrition was the most serious. Pirate crews ate whatever they could get their hands on. If they were lucky, they were able to put to shore frequently and barter for fresh provisions, or steal them if necessary; they might also be fortunate enough to attack ships that had plenty of good food. Indeed, pirates occasionally feasted on exotic delicacies and other special treats generally unavailable at sea. A pirate named William Dampier, for example, wrote of eating flamingos' tongues. Fresh fruits and vegetables were particularly good: "[We] found all fruits just ripe and fit for eating,"[31] noted Exquemelin about his band's journey to an island.

Pirates did have favorite dishes. A fish plate called salmagundi was especially popular. Though recipes varied, it included pickled herrings, chicken, spices, and fruits and vegetables. Pirates were also fond of sea tortoise, a delicacy easy enough to find in the Caribbean, and often enjoyed catching and eating wild goats on any of a number of islands around the world. "Our men feasted on shoar," wrote a no-longer starving pirate of the 1680s, "with Barbakude [barbecued] Goats and Fish &c."[32]

More often, though, buccaneers survived on a steady diet of sea biscuits, also known as hardtack, and fish and meat that had been dried and salted to keep it well preserved. Sometimes this diet was supplemented with freshly caught fish, lemons, and cheese. In either case, the fare soon grew monotonous. Worse, the food did not always last. Casks leaked, butter turned rancid, and vermin got into the rations. But unless there was an easy source of other food, pirates choked the stuff down anyway. "Weevils tasted bitter and made the throat feel dry," reported a seafarer experienced in such matters, "but maggots felt cold as they went down."[33]

In hard cases, moreover, pirates found themselves wishing for handfuls of weevily flour and wormy sea biscuits. Sometimes pirate crews had literally no food on board and no immediate chance of getting any. Esquemeling's crew was once reduced to cooking and eating leather. But even less desperate crews were not able to get the nutrients they needed to ward off diseases such as scurvy, a condition caused by lack of vitamin C and fresh foods. "We now have a very sickly ship," reported an English captain, "our men full of the scurvy."[34] No wonder; the menu on board that vessel consisted exclusively of water and flour with an occasional ration of chocolate or dried peas.

Life on board a pirate ship, therefore, was by turns boring, strenuous, and quite literally sickening—about as far from a romantic picture as can be imagined. It was a hard life, but one that a surprising number of sailors took up with enthusiasm. Given

Despite the wretched conditions on pirate ships, many pirates took up their lifestyle with enthusiasm.

the tenor of the times, piracy was a reasonable alternative for many men—including many who were not by nature sadistic, nor even especially greedy, as the stereotypical image has it. The pirates of the Golden Age did not exist in a vacuum; modern-day standards do not pertain to their decisions and their lives. To understand the Golden Age pirates and their impact on the world around them, it is necessary to look at these buccaneers in the context of their world.

3 Pirates and the World Around Them

Besides poor food, hard work, and awful living conditions, piracy also had one very significant disadvantage: What pirates were doing was by definition illegal, and so they were constantly subject to capture. Capture nearly always meant death, for piracy was a capital crime—that is, punishable by execution. The risks were high. Narratives of the period consistently mention pirates brought to court and sentenced to die. "The punishment for corsairs is to hang them in such a way that their toes well nigh touch the water," reported an Englishman who watched a pirate die in exactly this way. "They are generally hanged on the banks of rivers and on the sea-shore."[35] As the word *generally* suggests, the capture and subsequent execution of pirates was far from an uncommon occurrence. In November 1718 alone, forty-nine pirates were hanged in South Carolina.

Pirates, moreover, led dangerous lives. Battles and attacks were common enough, and many more pirates died violent deaths while trying to board another ship or while trying to evade pursuers. "Capt. Sawlkins was killd with 3 men more, to our greate sorrow,"[36] reported one pirate in a typical journal entry from 1682. Al-

though the records are perhaps somewhat biased—they tend not to discuss the pirates who were never caught—it is clear that piracy did represent a significant gamble.

Many pirates died violently while trying to board another vessel.

JOINING THE CREW

Sometimes it was difficult to tell whether a sailor had joined the crew of a pirate ship willingly or under duress. In 1717 Thomas Davis was arrested for piracy, but at his trial claimed that he had been forced to join when pirates attacked the merchant ship he was on. This account of the trial is quoted by J. Franklin Jameson in Privateering and Piracy in the Colonial Period.

"The said Ship was taken by two Pyrat Sloops, one comanded by Capt. Samuel Bellamy, and the other by Louis Le Boose. . . . [T]hey Gave the said Williams [Davis's captain] his Ship and Detained the Prisoner, because he was a Carpenter and a Singleman, together with Three others of the Ships Company. . . . [T]he Prisoner [that is, Davis] was very Unwilling to goe with Bellamy and prevailed with him by reason of his Intreatys [entreaties] to promise that he should be Discharged the next Vessell that was taken. . . .

[Another ship was taken some time later.] At which time the Pris'r reminded the said Bellamy of his promise. When he [Bellamy] asked him [Davis] if he was willing to goe he answered, yes, and then the said Capt. Bellamy replyed if the Company [that is, the whole crew] would Consent he should go. And thereupon he asked his Comp'y if they were willing to lett Davis the Carpenter go, Who Expressed themselves in a Violent manner saying no, Dam him, they would first shoot him or Whip him to Death at the Mast."

Why, then, would anyone choose this way of life? Today, the common stereotype of pirate crews is that most of them did not. Instead, they had piracy chosen for them. In the popular imagination, a few violent and greedy men set the tone for the period. These men used guns and the threat of violence to recruit crewmen onshore, and offered crews of ships captured at sea a choice between joining the buccaneers and being killed on the spot. Under such circumstances, the decision to join the pirates was usually no decision at all.

There is some truth to this image. Certainly a number of pirate crews included men forced aboard at gunpoint. Similarly, a few captains are known to have told their crews that they were sailing an ordinary merchant vessel, only revealing the truth after it was too late to return to port. Voyages often were organized in the bars of coastal towns, so it is quite likely that many pirate crewmen were drunk, or very nearly so, when they agreed to sign on. And the terror-inspiring aspect of some captains' personalities surely helped make up some prospective crewmen's minds. Blackbeard, for example, was said to have placed slow-burning matches in his twisted hair and to have commented once that "if he did not now and then kill one of [his crew members], they would forget who he was."[37]

But in fact most buccaneers knew perfectly well what they were getting themselves into, and most seemed to have made the choice to turn pirate of their own free will. In 1694, for example, the *Good Hope* of England was boarded by a pirate crew. The *Good Hope*'s master, Jeremiah Tay, described what happened next:

> After thay had posseshon of the Above said Shipe The next day sent for My Men. . . . Telling them that thoose as would goe willingly should have as good A shaar [share] in ships and goods as Anny [any] of themselves, whare upon one bengeman blackledg [Benjamin Blackledge, one of the crewmen] of boston, with sundry more [various others], tuck up armes with the pyrats. . . . This was dun by said blackledg without anny force or Compulshon, as the pyrats themselves did declare That they did not nor would not force him nor sundry more which did intend To goo with them.[38]

Some of the pirates of the Golden Age were drawn to piracy because they were adventurers at heart, and freebooting offered them a chance at an exciting and dramatic life. Others were motivated to turn pirate by dreams of great wealth. Still others were criminals already in trouble with the law for their actions on land. And

a few saw themselves as some sort of Robin Hood. "They rob the poor under the cover of law," said a pirate captain of the merchants and lords who ran England, "and we plunder the rich under the protection of our own courage."[39] For these people, their goals were worth the discomfort of long trips by sea, the constant danger of detection, and the possibility of violent death.

Still, other men with less clear-cut goals were also attracted to piracy. According to one study, the average pirate during the Golden Age seems to have been an unmarried man of about twenty-seven years of

Despite the presence of aristocrat pirates like Stede Bonnet (pictured), most pirates were members of the lower class.

age. By far the largest contingent of these pirates came from the lower classes, especially those from European cities serving as seaports. True, a few pirates such as William Kidd and Thomas Tew came from prosperous backgrounds. Contemporaries called sugar planter turned pirate Stede Bonnet "a gentleman that has had the Advantage of a liberal Education" and noted that he was "generally esteemed a Man of Letters."[40] Still, these men were exceptions: nearly all the buccaneers were poor.

The seventeenth and eighteenth centuries were difficult years to be impoverished and uneducated. Lacking skills, money, or social standing, these men found that the alternatives to piracy were few. Moreover, what alternatives there were seemed no more attractive than the realities of life aboard a pirate ship.

ALTERNATIVES

The Golden Age, after all, was hardly a golden age for anyone in developing countries but pirates—and the rich. Wealthy merchants and lords owned most of the land, forcing ordinary citizens onto small and unproductive farms. Commoners labored long hours in factories and mines for starvation wages. Competition for jobs was fierce. If one worker died, another was ready to take his place. There was no medical insurance, no Social Security, no offer of schooling for all. Most European nations had a rigid class system, and the opportunity for a poor person to advance was limited indeed.

For most of the men who became pirates, then, the lure of money was signifi-

cant. These men simply had no reasonable options if they wished to live a decent life. A factory worker or farmhand could never hope to save enough to escape the back-breaking labor and the endless hours of work. Indeed, many of these people had to borrow money to cover their monthly bills; some, unable to repay, were thrown into debtors' prison, where they might languish for the rest of their lives.

Life at sea paid little better. Naval sailors and merchant seamen earned slightly more than common laborers, but not nearly enough to make life at all comfortable. The contrast with piracy was striking. A pirate on a successful Golden Age cruise could make in one haul what a merchantman earned in a lifetime. In some cases, the money came to even more. To thousands of poorly paid sailors, farmers, and workers, piracy seemed the one path leading to wealth. But perhaps even more important, piracy was one of the few careers that could give them a living above subsistence level.

Nor were the living and working conditions aboard a pirate ship significantly worse than what these men would otherwise have experienced. The workload on merchant ships and naval vessels was every bit as brutal as the corresponding load aboard a pirate vessel. Sailors of every stripe had to scrub the decks, haul the gear, raise and lower anchors, and do all the other never-ending routine tasks of shipboard life. Likewise, men aboard law-abiding ships had to contend with rats, vermin, low rations, and other hazards that made life unpleasant or worse. Disease, malnutrition, and overwork were frequent. By some estimates, half of all seamen and common laborers in early-eighteenth-century

England failed to live beyond the age of thirty.

Those men who chose the legitimate sea trade also experienced discipline that was as harsh as anything on a pirate ship. Both naval and cargo vessels adhered to a rigid system of authority in which rank mattered enormously. The captains and officers held absolute sway over the ship. At best, the sailors had no authority in matters pertaining to the ship; at worst, they were subject to cruel punishments at the hands of tyrants. Some of the most vicious captains, in fact, were an unwitting source of pirates: they treated their crews so badly that the men mutinied, killed the officers—and then turned pirate rather than go back to shore and face the legal consequences of their actions.

In the context of the time, therefore, the brutality on pirate ships was not unusual. Inhuman tortures were the order of the day, on land as well as at sea. People could be hanged for stealing even a few pennies. Many of the worst buccaneer punishments were taken directly from practices common at the time and widely accepted. Indeed, many were derived from usual penalties meted out aboard naval ships and merchantmen. The pirate habit of tying murderers to the corpses of their victims and throwing them overboard, for example, was identical to the punishment the English navy gave murderers on its ships. And flogging was certainly a much more common punishment for naval men than it ever was on pirate ships.

To an ordinary lower-class citizen of the Golden Age, then, piracy seemed to be a reasonable career choice. Joining a pirate crew offered the prospect of wealth and power, commodities unavailable anywhere else. Buccaneers shared in the proceeds of their work; moreover, they had a say in the affairs of the ship. The drawbacks of shipboard life on a pirate vessel, while certainly significant, were far from unusual during the time. Punishment, working conditions, and creature comforts were not much different aboard merchant vessels or warships, let alone on land.

Indeed, pirate crews rarely forced men from other ships to join them. Except for a few skilled laborers—carpenters, surgeons, sail makers, and the like—there was no need to do so; recruits from conquered ships usually came willingly enough. "You have been serving a merchantman for twenty-five shillings a month," writes one commentator, summing up the pirate argument. "Here you may have seven or eight pounds a month."[41] Since a shilling was worth one-twentieth of a pound at the time, this was a persuasive case, especially if the captain of the ship had been even middlingly brutal. Some new recruits played it safe, however. They requested official documents from the pirates saying that they had been kidnapped; these might prove to be useful if the buccaneers were captured and tried for piracy. In most cases, the pirates were happy to oblige.

And why not? The pirate life, it seemed to some, held all the advantages. The notorious Bartholomew Roberts, one of the last pirates of the Golden Age, summed it up when he explained why he had chosen the pirate life:

In an honest Service there is thin Commons, low Wages and hard Labour; in

Although some sailors were forced to join pirate crews, most recruits, attracted by the potential for wealth, joined willingly.

this [that is, piracy] Plenty and Satiety, Pleasure and Ease, Liberty and Power. [A]nd who would not balance Creditor on [decide in favor of] this Side when all the Hazard that is run for it, at worst, is only a forelock or two at choaking [that is, when the possibility of hanging is the only drawback].[42]

MERCHANTS, POLITICIANS, AND COASTAL TOWNS

Pirates made use of those around them to enlist new recruits, but they also made good use of many people who did not ever join their ranks. During the Golden Age, the buccaneers often received help, both secretive and obvious, from the citizens of seafaring communities. The merchants who bought the pirate loot, the politicians who turned a blind eye, and the hangers-on who provided a buffer from the authorities—all of these helped make the Golden Age a time of unparalleled success for pirates. In some ways, these people were even more useful to the pirates in these capacities than they would have been had they joined the crews.

The Golden Age may have gotten its start on several out-of-the-way islands of the

MERCHANTS AND PIRATES

This ledger sheet describes some of the materials traded between New York's respected businessman Frederick Philipse and pirates in the Indian Ocean, as quoted by Douglas Botting in The Pirates.

"26 barrils of beer at 60 ps8 [pieces of eight] p[e]r barril
15 barrils of wine at 60 ps8 pr barril
 2 pipes of wine 100 a pipe
72 gall[ons] of wine
927 gall & 1/2 of rum at 4 ps8 $ 1/2 pr gall
10 Barrils of Salt at 15 ps8 pr barrill
10 Barrils of peace [peas] at 20 ps8 pr barril
10 dozens of black hafted knives 1/2 a p8 a knive
12 Shoemakers knives at 1 ps8 1/2 pr knive
 1 dozen of thimbles
20 dozen 1/2 of Sizars [scissors] 1 ps8 a paire
 6 Pound $ 1/2 of thread
1/4 of a pound ditto
 6 pound Colloured [colored] thread
 6 dozen of horn Combs
 2 dozen & 1/2 of Ivory Combs 2 ps8 pr Com[b]
 2 piar taylors [tailor's] Sizars
3000 Needles"

West Indies, but the very nature of piracy dictated that it not remain localized. Pirates needed markets—places to spend their loot and trade it in for cash or other valuables. Given the lawless frontier atmosphere of the Caribbean, the political conflicts between the Spanish and others, and the lack of any real police presence in the area, that was not hard. Pirates soon found merchants on nearby bigger islands who were willing to deal with them. As pirates became more numerous and more powerful, too, they increasingly threatened those merchants who would not; most eventually gave in and dealt with the pirates on their terms.

Pirates were able to increase their influence, too, by involving themselves in the clash between the Spanish and their enemies. By 1660, for example, the island of Jamaica was technically in English hands. However, it had been only thinly settled by England. The few sugar planters, merchants, and various others were not nearly enough to keep the Spanish at bay should they decide to reclaim the island. Knowing the situation, some enterprising buccaneers offered the colonial government a deal. The government would officially ignore some of the pirates' most flagrant abuses of the law, and in exchange the pirates would help defend the island from Spanish forces. Better yet, the pirates would bring their treasures to Jamaica and spend money on the island, thus giving the local economy an important boost. The governors eagerly accepted, and the system proved valuable to both sides. "It is to the buccaneers that we owe possession of Jamaica to this hour,"[43] wrote an English historian in 1774.

Such bargains, struck between the buccaneers and the English, Dutch, and French interlopers, eventually led to a succession of pirate bases across the Caribbean. In these towns and islands, pirates held most of the power and did as they chose. Port Royal, Jamaica, was probably the best known of these bases. Run by an openly pro-pirate governor, it was a true pirate haven. As one historian describes it, with the advent of the pirates, the sleepy, sparsely populated community "became, in no time at all, a bustling port town complete with strumpets and wine, gaming tables and ale houses, and even a church or two."[44] Port Royal, however, was simply one of several such towns that sprang up early in the Golden Age to supply and support the pirates.

Because they gave local economies a boost, pirates were often welcomed in many coastal towns. Here, a group of drunken pirates revel in Charleston, South Carolina.

The connection between pirates and these communities was astonishingly tight. Merchants openly bought and sold pirated goods, and other businesses relied on wealthy pirates coming to town and being free with their money. The townspeople were rarely disappointed. "They spend prodigally," remarked one observer of the pirates, "giving themselves to all manner of vice and debauchery, particularly to drunkenness, which they practiced mostly with brandy."[45] In late-seventeenth-century Port Royal, for example, the population of about six thousand people supported at least nineteen pubs.

To the Pacific and Indian Oceans

As pirates pushed outward into new territory, new frontier settlements sprang up to take the place of Port Royal and other pirate havens like it. Some of these had previously been only lightly populated, and a few had not been settled at all. The Juan Fernández islands off the Chilean coast, for example, served a useful purpose for the pirates; for many years they provided seafarers with fresh water, milk and meat from wild goats, and fresh fish and vegetables.

The Indian Ocean island of Madagascar, near the coast of southern Africa, became an even more impressive pirate base. Indeed, Madagascar was settled more or less permanently by several hundred buccaneers. It also afforded protection and supplies to countless others. As one historian writes:

The first rendezvous of the pirates was in Masseledge Bay on the northwest coast of Madagascar, but later an important settlement grew up on the island of St. Mary, or Nosy Boraha, on the east coast, about three leagues from the mainland. . . . The island stronghold was established, it is said, by [pirate captains] Mission and Carracioli, who named it Libertaria. It was fortified and from here marauding [looting] expeditions were fitted out on a grand scale. Pirates gorged with plunder settled on plantations where they surrounded themselves with native "wives" and slaves.[46]

Not all of these new pirate havens were sparsely populated. Some carried on in the tradition of Port Royal. New Providence in the Bahamas, just outside the Caribbean itself, became known for its friendliness to pirates and other "loose disorderly People."[47] The governor himself was said to have been an ex-pirate. Several ports in what is now the United States opened their arms to the pirates, too, notably Charleston, South Carolina, which one historian has called "a second Jamaica."[48]

As had been true in the Caribbean, moreover, pirates quickly gained friends in high places. Many people in the American colonies gave more or less obvious aid to the pirates. Well-heeled and otherwise honest merchants, coveting the treasures the pirates took in, provided ships, men, and supplies in exchange for a share of the proceeds. Colonial governors winked at the trade, too, rationalizing—as had been

MADAGASCAR

Robert Drury, an Englishman, visited a pirate settlement on Madagascar in 1716. There he met a former pirate named John Pro. His description of Pro is quoted by George Francis Dow and John Henry Edmonds in The Pirates of the New England Coast, 1630–1739.

"John Pro lived in a very handsome manner. His house was furnished with pewter dishes, &c., a standing bed with curtains, and other things of that nature except chairs, but a chest or two served for that purpose well enough. He had one house on purpose for his cook-room and cook-slave's lodging, storehouse and summerhouse; all these were enclosed in a palisade, as the great men's houses are in this country [that is, England], for he was rich, and had many castles and slaves. His wealth had come principally while cruizzing among the Moors, from whom his ship had several times taken great riches, and used to carry it to St. Mary's. But their ship growing old and crazy, they also being vastly rich, they removed to Madagascar, made one Thomas Collins, a carpenter, their Governor, and built a small fort, defending it with their ship's guns. They had now lived without pirating for nine years."

done in Port Royal—that pirates were ultimately good for the local economy. Pirates only were brought to court if they had made major blunders. Even then not-guilty verdicts were the order of the day.

The extent of the cooperation between pirates and those onshore was remarkable. In North Carolina, the notorious Blackbeard paid off the governor in exchange for judicial immunity for his actions. In Boston, the community provided pilots to guide the buccaneers in and out of the harbor. A New York merchant named Frederick Philipse was a respected member of the colonial government, a landowner—and an open supporter of piracy who sent out ships to Madagascar to buy pirate booty and supply the pirate crews with necessary materials.

Moreover, the wealthy at all levels benefited from piracy. As one historian sums up:

> A lady connected with shareholders of shipping enterprises dealing with pirates might well relish her petticoats woven with (stolen) cotton and gowns of (stolen) brocade. Her morning beverage might be (stolen) cocoa, her evening tipple [drink] (stolen) Madeira or Portuguese wine. Her maid could tie her hair with ribbon

dyed by (stolen) indigo and dream of the (stolen) silver in the storeroom. And her cook could spice her winter meat with (stolen) cardamom and her summer apple pie with (stolen) cloves.[49]

Piracy, quite simply, made the lives of the rich easier by providing them with goods at much lower prices than they would otherwise have to pay—assuming that the goods could have been obtained legally at all.

During the Golden Age, then, it was perhaps not surprising that pirates should have had such close connections to the communities around them. The merchants, governors, and landowners who settled in colonial America and on Caribbean islands had good reasons to support the buccaneers. Their own pockets were enriched by pirate activities, and their communities grew more stable as a result of the buccaneers and their work. In return, they were happy to overlook the fact that the pirates broke the law, and even the truth that they

FRIENDLY OFFICIALS

Government officials in the Caribbean often won praise at home for their willingness to encourage the pirates, especially when those pirates seemed most likely to act in the interests of their nation. This character sketch of a French governor, quoted in History of the Buccaneers of America *by James Burney, is typical.*

"Besides encouraging the cultivation of lands, he never neglected to encourage the Flibustiers [pirates]. It was a certain means of improving the Colony, by attracting thither the young and enterprising. He would scarcely receive a slight portion of what he was entitled to from his right of bestowing commissions in time of war [for privately owned ships to attack enemy merchant vessels. A tenth of the proceeds of these attacks was to go to the government. The implication is that he offered the pirates most of his share as well in order to give them a further incentive to come to his territory]. And when we were at peace, and our Flibustiers, for want of other employment, would go cruising, and would carry their prizes to the English Islands, he was at the pains of procuring them commissions from Portugal, which country was then at war with Spain [and was therefore friendly to France]; in virtue of which our Flibustiers continued to make themselves redoubtable [threatening] to the Spaniards, and to spread riches and abundance in our Colonies."

could be exceedingly violent at times. As Rudyard Kipling wrote many years later about a town that benefited from maritime smuggling:

Five and twenty ponies,

Trotting through the dark—

Brandy for the parson,

'Baccy [tobacco] for the Clerk.

Them that asks no questions isn't told a lie—

Watch the wall, my darling, while the Gentlemen go by![50]

The shoreline communities of America and the West Indies were quite willing to "watch the wall" while the "gentlemen" did their business.

4 Pirates and Their Victims

It takes two to make a pirate. Not only must there be a thief with a ship and the desire to take property by force, but there also must be a victim: a property owner who becomes the target of the raider. At most times through history, piracy has been limited enough to allow most people to avoid its ravages. A ship's captain who stayed away from a particularly dangerous zone would probably avoid attack, for example. During the Golden Age, however, things changed. Across much of the world, virtually no one in a coastal port or aboard a seagoing vessel was entirely safe from the pirates. The story of these victims is a central part of the story of the pirates.

PIRATE VICTIMS

The Golden Age began with a particular focus on capturing Spanish goods. Part of this focus was based on the long-standing rivalries between Spain and its enemies in Europe, but more of it stemmed from the fact that the Spanish ships offered the greatest chance of booty. Likewise, plundering Spanish ports turned out to be extremely profitable. The Englishman Christopher Myngs, for instance, captured a ton of sil-ver on just one raid to Venezuela in 1659, and eight years later a French buccaneer known as L'Ollonais collected more than a quarter million pieces of eight from the inhabitants of two Central American towns settled by the Spanish.

But by the middle of the seventeenth century, the Spanish were no longer the only victims of pirates. Other nations were transporting gold, silver, silks, and spices as well, and their ships were often easier to find and capture. In 1704 the English Parliament bemoaned:

> That certain Pyrates having some Years since found the Island of Madagascar to be the most Proper, if not the only Place in the World for their Abode, and carrying on their Destructive Trade with Security, betook themselves thither; and being since increased to a formidable Body are become a manifest Obstruction to Trade. . . . [51]

Of course, pirates had long since become a "manifest obstruction to trade"; England was only beginning to notice, however, as the pirates were increasingly attacking without discriminating among the national origins of ships. English pirates attacked English ships; the Dutch attacked the Dutch. "Most of them [are] English," Parliament pointed out ruefully, "at least four Fifths."

As piracy became more of a worldwide phenomenon, too, ships belonging to non-European nations also began to be attacked. This was especially noticeable in the case of ships belonging to the Great Mogul (emperor) of India. India had been unified under Muslim rule since the early sixteenth century. Ever since then, trading ships had traveled the waters of the Indian Ocean and the Red Sea, carrying goods to various parts of the Islamic world. There had been some specifically Asian pirates who had preyed on the fleet—and on

RANSOM

Pirates were just as likely to attack coastal settlements as ships at sea. The French pirate François L'Ollonais, for example, attacked a Spanish town in present-day Venezuela and took many prisoners, some of whom he and his crew tortured to death. L'Ollonais's doings are described in The Buccaneers of America *by Alexander Exquemelin.*

". . . After having been in possession of the town four entire weeks, [the pirates] sent four of the prisoners, remaining alive, to the Spaniards that fled into the woods, demanding of them a ransom for not burning the town. The sum hereof they constituted *ten thousand pieces of eight*, which, unless it were sent to them, they threatened to fire and reduce into ashes the whole village. For bringing in of this money they allowed them only the space of two days. These being past, and the Spaniards not having been able to gather so punctually such a sum, the Pirates began to set fire to many places of the town. Thus the inhabitants, perceiving the Pirates to be in earnest, begged of them to help to extinguish the fire; and withal promised the ransom should be readily paid. The Pirates condescended to their petition, helping as much as they could to stop the progress of the fire. Yet, though they used the best endeavours they possibly could, one part of the town was ruined, especially the church belonging to the monastery, which was burnt even to dust. . . . Hence they returned to Maracaibo [a nearby town that they had attacked some time earlier], where being arrived they found a general consternation in the whole city. To which they sent three or four prisoners to tell the governor and inhabitants: *They should bring them thirty thousand pieces of eight on board their ships, for a ransom of their houses; otherwise they should be entirely sacked anew and burnt.*"

other European ships that wandered into harm's way. Most notable among these was a band of buccaneers led by Kanhoji Angria at the end of the seventeenth century.

But it did not take long for European pirates to join in. Pirates from Denmark, the Netherlands, and other European nations were recorded in the Red Sea as far back as the early part of the 1600s, and Thomas Tew began a run on Mogul shipping by capturing a huge prize in the 1690s. The Indian ships were profitable targets. They carried gold, silver, silks, and other valuables; one pirate commented that money in the Red Sea was "as plenty as stones or sand."[52]

The Indian ships were also relatively easy to catch. The Mogul Empire was in decline, and the emperor was unable to spend as much as he wanted for protection, or to outfit better and faster ships. Better yet, the ships belonged to Muslims, considered religious enemies by Christian pirates; thus, there was little moral dilemma in plundering them. "In eighteenth-century trials," writes a historian, "Anglo-American pirates [who attacked Indian ships] usually said they did not consider themselves to be sinners: many felt they were acting for their Christian God and King against the infidels."[53]

STOPPING THE PIRATES

Merchants and governments took several measures to stop the pirates. Even the smallest ships usually carried a few guns, which were traditionally mounted on the side of the vessel behind open areas known as gun ports. Where they could, merchants added firepower and extra crewmen to their fleets, the better to ward off the buccaneers. However, doing so cut into their profits. As one historian points out with regard to the British East India Company, which lost many ships to piracy during the Golden Age,

> The chances were better than fifty-fifty that an underarmed and under-crewed East Indiaman would get through and make a big profit, while the chances were absolutely 100 percent that a properly armed and properly crewed vessel would *lose* money. The only sensible course open to the company was to take the fifty-fifty bet and continue to operate its ships with too little armament and too few crewmen.[54]

Where merchants chose not to add extra men and guns, they often had extra gun ports painted on the sides to give the illusion of strength. In areas known to be infested by pirates, lookouts were told to be especially careful in scanning the seas, and some merchants took the time and money to make sure their ships were in the best possible condition, thus increasing speed and durability. Still, the cost of these measures sometimes outweighed the possible profit, and so many merchants skimped here as well.

Some companies required their ships to travel in groups. The Spanish had originated this maneuver early in the Golden Age, perhaps even before; by the beginning of the 1700s, the strategy was well known

*In order to protect their precious cargo, Spanish ships often made the
perilous journey to Spain in convoys.*

throughout all shipping nations. In 1707, for example, England required all its ships cruising between Virginia and Britain to travel with others, and in 1711 a handful of English ships refused to leave southern Africa until joined by a convoy of Dutch vessels. Once in a while an especially daring or foolhardy pirate would attack a fleet of merchant ships—Bartholomew Roberts once took twenty-two ships with one attack, and there were other examples. Still, as a rule there was safety in numbers.

Often, though not always, the formation of convoys was done in conjunction with governments. The Spanish again introduced this custom. Concerned about the steady loss of valuables into the hands of enemies, Spain was already sending armed guards along with merchant ships during the sixteenth century. Later on, England and other nations began to do the same. Unfortunately, the system was rife with corruption, as a historian explains:

> By Admiralty law, Navy commanders were allowed to charge 12 1/2 percent of the value of the cargo they were escorting on convoy duty. When a merchant complained about the resulting freight charges, the Navy commanders offered a sub rosa [secret] deal: they

Dying Apologies

In 1724 John Archer was hanged in Boston for piracy. Before he died, he dictated a declaration to a minister, quoted by George Francis Dow and John Henry Edmonds in The Pirates of the New England Coast, 1630–1730. *Part apology and part explanation, Archer blamed himself for his crimes, but he also laid some blame on the treatment of sailors in merchant and naval fleets.*

"I Greatly bewail my Profanations of the Lord's Day, and my Disobedience to my Parents. And my Cursing and Swearing, and my blaspheming the Name of the glorious God.

Unto which I have added, the Sins of Unchastity. And I have provoked the Holy One, at length, to leave me unto the Crimes of Pyracy and Robbery; wherein, at last, I have brought my self under the Guilt of Murder also.

But one Wickedness that has led me as much as any, to all the rest, has been my brutish Drunkenness. By strong Drink I have been heated and hardened into the Crimes that are now more bitter than Death unto me.

I could wish that Masters of Vessels would not use their Men with so much Severity, as many of them do, which exposes us to great Temptations."

would transport the goods in their own ships and charge less than the cargo vessels. This was illegal, of course, but profitable to most of those concerned. The pirates did not attack the Navy-escorted convoys and the Navy did not attack the pirates, who were thus free to concentrate on un-protected shipping.[55]

Moreover, charging for the guards in-flated the price of the goods and ulti-mately lessened the wealth of the nation.

None of these strategies was especially effective against a determined pirate. Individual action, in fact, was generally of little value. If one ship was well armed, the pirates would scarcely be put out of

business: they would simply add to their own armaments and attack a less well-protected vessel. If one group of ships had an escort, that, too, was acceptable to the pirates, who would simply cruise until they came upon one that did not—as they invariably would. It would take more concerted efforts on the part of mer-chants—and most of all, governments—before the pirate threat was brought under control.

Stalking Prey

Indeed, through most of the Golden Age, it was easy enough for pirate captains to capture their prey. Most of the time they could overcome a target without resorting to violence. One reason was speed. Pirate ships were almost invariably fast; if they were not, the crew would try to obtain a different, swifter ship. A fast ship enabled pirates to catch up to their prey and to wait for just the right moment before attacking. Knowing they could not outrun the buccaneers, many captains of merchant ships were quick to give up and accept the inevitable.

The element of surprise was important, too, and pirates gave themselves this edge as well. They preferred ships with a shallow draft—that is, ships that required very little water in order to maneuver properly.

As a result, pirates were able to make excellent use of coves, river mouths, and islands. A merchant ship crew might not suspect that a pirate ship lurked behind a stand of trees; so much the better for the pirates, who could attack unexpectedly, before the merchants were prepared to put up resistance.

Finally, tactics played a role. Pirates made it their business to know their territory. As a result, they had information that the merchant vessels passing through could not have had, especially in a time of poor maps. The pirates, for example, knew the direction and intensity of the prevailing winds, which allowed them to anticipate the course of the ships as they came

Fast sailing and very maneuverable, the brigantine (pictured) was the ship of choice for many pirate crews.

near. Similarly, they knew where the waters were shallow and where they were deep, which enabled them to push their prey toward dangerous reefs and rocks; rather than run aground, merchant captains sometimes surrendered.

The buccaneers made use of other strategies as well. Attacking at dawn or at dusk was especially common. Not only would the merchant crew have trouble seeing the pirates approach, but any guard ships in the vicinity might miss the attack altogether. Keeping masts low served a similar purpose: a pirate vessel could come quite near its prey, even during the day, without being noticed. Both strategies kept pirates out of immediate danger while permitting them to decide from up close whether an attack was worthwhile. The questions were many: What was the ship likely to be carrying? How fast did it seem? What nationality did it claim? Were those real gun ports on the sides, or were they only painted on? If the answers to the questions were favorable to an attack, the pirates were already in an excellent position to make the attempt; if the answers indicated a retreat, there was little danger of discovery and no harm done.

Positioning was of critical importance as well. Pirates had a few guns mounted on the sides of their ships, but rarely did they have enough to match the firepower of a merchant, let alone a naval vessel. A pirate ship that sailed alongside a possible victim risked being shot to pieces. Thus, pirate captains were careful to approach an opponent from the stern, or the rear of the ship. It was impractical to mount many guns on the stern, so the pirates

were safe enough as long as they did not allow their prey to turn quickly.

Faced with these disadvantages, most merchant captains surrendered the moment the pirates made themselves known, or at least as soon as the pirates fired an opening shot. Too often, putting up a fight would have been suicidal. Outmanned and outmaneuvered, most captains had little chance of winning. But a few thought it was worth a try. Indeed, occasionally it was. Sometimes a lucky shot from the rear would damage the pirate ship so severely its crew elected to call off the attack. Sometimes the wind would change abruptly, giving the victim a chance to escape. Sometimes a nearby ship would hear or see the commotion and

A pirate ship explodes after being hit by cannon fire. Occasionally, merchant ships were able to fend off a pirate attack.

come to the aid of the merchant, frightening off the pirate crew.

Usually, however, the pirates won any battle they chose to engage in. By the end of the Golden Age, in fact, the buccaneers were so feared that help from a fellow merchant ship was rare. Even when ships were specifically sent out to attack pirates, help was not always forthcoming. In 1720, for instance, the *Cassandra* was attacked by two pirate ships in the Indian Ocean. The *Cassandra*'s captain, James Macrae, called for help from a nearby ship, the *Greenwich*. Although the two ships were traveling together and had both been assigned to hunt down pirates, Captain Kirby of the *Greenwich* refused to help. Instead, he quickly sailed away and watched the fight from a safe distance. Macrae fought bravely and actually gained a distinct advantage at one point in the battle, but even then Kirby refused to join the fight. Two against one proved to be overwhelming odds, and Macrae lost his ship, most of his crew, and very nearly his life. Afterward Macrae was bitter, saying of his fellow captain:

> He basely [dishonorably] deserted us, and left us engaged with barbarous and inhuman enemies with their Black and Bloody flags hanging over us and no appearance of escaping being cut to pieces. . . . [A]s we had considerable advantage [later in the battle] by having our broadside to his bow I believe we should have taken both, for we had this one sure, had Captain Kirby then come in.[56]

Kirby's actions are hard to defend, but his decision to avoid battle at all costs does indicate how feared the pirates of the time actually were.

TREATMENT OF ENEMIES

If pirates could be brutal to their fellow shipmates, they often behaved far worse where their enemies were concerned. As a contemporary said of the pirate Edward Low, Low "took a small vessel . . . [to] declare War against all the World."[57] The ranks of pirates included some men who took pleasure in hurting others, and many others for whom torture of captives soon became a way of life. While pirates did not treat all prisoners viciously, they brutalized more than enough people to give themselves a well-deserved reputation for wanton violence and vengeful cruelty.

The various tortures used by pirates were often appallingly diabolical. Henry Morgan's men, for example, decided to browbeat a Panamanian into giving them the location of valuables. "They first put him upon the rack," wrote a chronicler, "wherewith they inhumanly disjointed his arms. After this, they twisted a cord about his forehead, which they wrung so hard, that his eyes appeared as big as eggs, and were ready to fall out of his skull."[58] When these measures failed, the pirates hung the poor fellow upside down, beat him unmercifully, cut off his nose and his ears, and eventually burned what remained of his face, all to no avail. Frustrated and still no closer to the loot, the pirates eventually had him run through with a lance, killing him.

BARBARITY

English pirate Henry Morgan and his men were determined to find where an old Portuguese man had hidden his valuables. As Alexander Exquemelin describes in The Buccaneers of America, *Morgan's crew had been told that the man was extremely wealthy.*

"This man was commanded to produce his riches. But his answer was, he had no more than one hundred pieces of eight in the whole world, and that these had been stolen from him two days before, by a servant of his. Which words, although he sealed with many oaths and protestations, yet they would not believe him. But dragging him to the rack, without any regard to his age, as being threescore years old, they stretched him with cords, breaking both his arms behind his shoulders.

This cruelty went not alone. For he not being able or willing to make any other declaration than the above-said, they put him to another sort of torment that was worse and more barbarous than the preceding. They tied him with small cords by his two thumbs and great-toes to four stakes that were fixed in the ground at a convenient distance, the whole weight of his body being pendent in the air upon those cords. Then they thrashed upon the cords with great sticks and all their strength, so that the body of this miserable man was ready to perish at every stroke, under the severity of these horrible pains. Not satisfied as yet with this cruel torture, they took a stone which weighed above two hundred pounds, and laid it on his belly, as if they intended to press him to death. At which time they also kindled palm-leaves, and applied the flame to the face of this unfortunate Portuguese, burning with them the whole skin, beard and hair.

[The man survived, though barely; he promised to raise one thousand pieces of eight from among his friends, which he did, and] got his liberty; although so horribly maimed in his body, that 'tis scarce to be believed he could survive many weeks after."

Henry Morgan became notorious not only for his exploits but also for his cruelty toward his prisoners.

Such stories were common enough. In an anti-Catholic religious frenzy, a seventeenth-century Dutch pirate fleet tore open the abdomen of a friar at a Caribbean monastery and forced him to watch as his inner organs spilled out. Vicious captains sewed prisoners' lips together. Crewmen tied their captives to ship masts, threw broken bottles at them, and then sank the ship. One notorious killer bundled several captives inside a sail and dumped the sail overboard with the helpless men inside. Where enemies were concerned, life was cheap.

Not all captives were subject to these particularly horrifying punishments, however. Some captains and crews were kinder than others, although "kind" is a relative term with regard to pirate tortures. Sometimes, too, pirates were in a relatively good mood after capturing prisoners. This was especially true if the merchant they attacked had put up little resistance, or if a prize had turned out to be particularly valuable. In such cases, pirates might release those captives who did not choose to join the crew, occasionally even sending them away with a share of the loot. After a few weeks of being held prisoner by a pirate band, for example, merchant captain William Snelgrave was allowed to go home—with a ship, part of his cargo, and many thousand pounds of goods belonging to the pirate crew. The pirates even gave him a farewell party and helped him transfer materials to his new ship.

But not all captives were equal. Pirate crews reserved particular fury for several categories of prisoner. Most obvious, perhaps, were naval officers who had been sent to stop the pirates in the first place.

The punishment pirate crews inflicted on prisoners was often cruel and sadistic.

Their success meant the end of the pirates' careers and very likely their lives as well, and so captured officers were often the victims of truly macabre penalties. There was brutality in the pirates' response, to be sure, but there was a strong streak of self-preservation as well. "The buccaneers may have been motivated by treasure," explains a historian, "but they were *always* fighting for their lives."[59] Torturing those who tried to hunt them down was one way of staying in business—and staving off death.

Another group that suffered especially at the hands of pirates included those who hid valuables from them—or, at least, those whom the pirates suspected of hiding valuables. Many of the pirates' worst atrocities were deliberate attempts to extract confessions from suspects: Unable to find loot they were sure must exist, pirates determined to torture someone who might know. Sometimes they were right. Just as often, however, they found and tortured a victim who was ignorant of the hiding place. Alternatively, the pirates discovered in the end that there was no treasure at all.

A third group coming in for particular punishment consisted of certain merchant captains. Pirates were always eager to trade their ship in for a newer, sleeker, and faster model. Knowing this, some captains did their best to point out their ships' flaws, hoping to convince the buccaneers to at least leave them their ships. That was a dangerous strategy. Those found to have lied about the sailing capacities of their

While some crews attempted to defend themselves against pirate attacks, many others, fearing pirates' reputations for brutality, surrendered without a fight.

ships were severely punished. Similarly, captains who had been unfair and brutal disciplinarians on their own ship were often tortured by pirates eager to punish dictatorial rule. "If you tell the truth, and your men make no complaints against you, you shall be kindly used [well treated]," William Snelgrave was told when the pirates commandeered his ship. If not, however, he would be "cut to pieces."[60]

Pirates of the Golden Age enjoyed their vicious reputation. Indeed, they encouraged the notion that they were brutal and dangerous. Not all of the reported atrocities were entirely accurate, but pirates rarely complained. "Many stories told how we murdered the people in cold blood," wrote a pirate, "one half of which, however, was not true."[61] Partly this was because the macho culture of pirate ships valued displays of violence: Taking prisoners could become a contest in which each pirate strove to prove himself meaner than his fellow crewmen.

But the image of the bloodthirsty pirate fueled the pirates' success as well. It may have been dramatic and exciting to stage an attack on a merchant ship, but it was also dangerous. Pirates could be injured, maimed, or killed in the fighting, and the buccaneers could ultimately lose the battle. Thus, while pirates were usually willing to fight, they preferred not to. The pirates were better off if the merchant simply surrendered upon seeing the pirates approach. Many merchant captains chose exactly this path, fearing that any resistance would push the pirates into a reign of terror once the battle was lost. A reputation for violence and torture therefore worked in the pirates' favor by making their jobs easier. As one historian writes:

> Force was far from their favored way to gain an objective. They were well aware of what can happen to a man in a naval battle—the effect of a shower of oak splinters, flying like six-inch daggers; the butchery of the ship's surgeon or carpenter; the horror of gangrene in the tropics. They were not in any regular armed service; they were not fighting for King and Country or abstract causes or because they had to. They saw no reason to risk their lives for something they could not enjoy if they were dead.[62]

5 Pirates and Privateers

The British explorer and seaman Francis Drake is remembered today as a heroic figure. Drake's list of accomplishments is indeed great. He helped lead the British fleet against the Spanish Armada in 1588, destroying the great Spanish navy and ushering in an era of English dominion over the seas. He was the first Englishman—and one of the first seafarers of any nation—to make a voyage around the entire globe, thus adding tremendously to European geographic knowledge. He was involved in colonial expansion, and his dash and verve as a sea captain inspired generations of adventurers—and delighted generations of armchair travelers as well. For his efforts, Drake was knighted.

Hero Drake may well have been—but there is more to his story than that. Indeed, in many of his actions Drake behaved remarkably like a pirate. Throughout his trip around the world, Drake harassed the merchant ships of Spain whenever possible. In some cases, moreover, he went out of his way to find them. Off the western coast of South America, for example, Drake overcame a Spanish ship that was carrying nearly two hundred pounds of gold. His crew drew up alongside, boarded the Spanish ship, and relieved its men of their cargo.

Believing that the ship's clerk was hiding some of the gold from them, too, Drake nearly hanged the clerk. Only when it became clear that his ignorance of more gold was real did Drake relent; instead, he had the clerk dropped into the sea, which did not kill him.

This was only one of several piratical acts Drake's crew would commit. Soon after this capture, Drake came upon a Spanish ship carrying twenty-six tons of silver, along with gold, jewels, and other precious metals from the New World. This time Drake not only took the booty, but very nearly destroyed the ship in the bargain. By the time he was through, the Spanish vessel had virtually no masts remaining. Nor was this journey the only one in which Drake took up a piratical outlook. A few years after this one, Drake voyaged to the Caribbean and resumed piracy, although this time with a little less success than he had enjoyed before.

HERO OR VILLAIN, PIRATE OR PRIVATEER

Whether people viewed Drake as a hero or a villain depended entirely on politics.

That English-speaking countries consider Drake a hero today is entirely the result of politics. What Drake did furthered the interests of his country. Instead of plundering for the sake of plunder, or attacking ships of whatever nation happened along, Drake was a patriotic Englishman who was careful to set his sights exclusively on the ships of Spain. Since England and Spain were hostile toward each other during most of Drake's time as a captain, Drake was helping the English each time he attacked a Spanish galleon.

Ideally, Drake's attacks would succeed in diverting Spanish wealth from the coffers of the Spanish king to the English treasury. Ideally, too, his raids would strike fear into the hearts of Spanish captains everywhere. But even if the ships he attacked were carrying little in the way of valuables, Drake's piracy still served an important purpose. Any harassment of the Spanish would irritate the Spanish government, unnerve Spanish merchant captains, and force the Spanish to spend more money than they might like on trying to protect their treasure ships.

Queen Elizabeth I knighted Francis Drake partly because of his numerous privateering adventures against the Spanish.

FRANCIS DRAKE AND HIS CREW, ACCORDING TO A SPANIARD

In April 1579 Francis Drake and his crew took a Spanish vessel belonging to a man named Francisco de Zarate. As quoted in Kris E. Lane's Pillaging the Empire, *Zarate described Drake and his crew with surprising appreciation, given how he had come to meet them.*

"He is called Francisco Drak, and is a man of about 35 years of age, low of stature, with a fair beard, and is one of the greatest mariners that sails the seas, both as a navigator and as a commander. His vessel is . . . a perfect sailer. She is manned with a hundred men, all of service and of an age for warfare, and all are as practiced therein as old soldiers could be. Each one takes particular pains to keep his arquebus [type of gun] clean. He treats them with affection and they treat him with respect. He carries with him nine or ten cavaliers, cadets of English noblemen. These form a part of his council, which he calls together for even the most trivial matter, although he takes advice from no one. But he enjoys hearing what they say and afterwards issues his orders. . . . He is served on silver dishes with gold borders and gilded garlands, in which are his arms [that is, his coat of arms]. He carries all possible dainties and perfumed waters. . . . He dines and sups to the music of viols."

Francis Drake was both feared and admired by many Spanish captains.

To the Spanish, on the other hand, Drake was a pirate, pure and simple. He acted like a pirate, he stole like a pirate, he used terror like a pirate: therefore, he was one. It did not matter that political reasons were behind his raids. To the English, however, Drake's efforts at piracy were not only approved by the highest levels of English government: more than that, Drake was formally under contract with his country to do what he did.

Instead of using the term *pirate*, then, English observers of the time used a different word: *privateer*. A pirate was someone to avoid, a bloodthirsty tyrant of a man, but a privateer was a man who loved his country, a man who deserved the attention and respect given a naval commander. The fact that pirates and privateers were often indistinguishable in their behavior did not matter: the two were considered separate and far from equivalent. "Judged by the standards of [the twentieth] century," sums up a historian, Drake and other privateers "were pirates . . . but in the eyes of their fellow-countrymen their attacks upon the Spaniards seemed fair and honourable."[63]

Privateers have been active in every age. Indeed, many of the people who went pirating often started their pirate careers aboard privateering vessels, or moved from piracy to privateering instead. The pirates of fourteenth-century northern Europe were privateers as often as not. So were many of the men who pillaged during Roman times. Nearly every war involving navies has seen privateering expeditions. Among the best-recorded privateers of history, however, two groups stand out: the English, Dutch, and French raiders of the early Golden Age and the period just before it, and the American privateers of the Revolutionary War.

COMMISSIONS AND LETTERS OF MARQUE

On the surface, the distinction between pirate and privateer was clear and straightforward. Like Drake, a privateer had the express backing of his government. This backing was usually done in the form of a written contract, known as a commission or as a letter of marque. The document permitted the privateer to take plunder from certain ships or to attack certain ports. One given by the king of Portugal in 1658, for example, authorized the holder to "wage warr with the subjects of the Kinge of spaine, Turks, Pirats, [and] Sea Roavers."[64] Although the holder of the letter of marque was a private citizen, the letter enabled him to act as a representative of the nation itself in attacking ships.

However, privateers were strictly limited to the terms of their commissions. During the American Revolution, for example, prospective captains were required to post bonds of anywhere from five to ten

An American privateer destroys a merchant vessel. Unlike pirates, privateers had the consent of their governments to attack the merchant vessels of enemy nations.

thousand dollars before being permitted to leave on a privateering voyage. These bonds could be forfeited if captains did not follow their commissions to the letter. The last thing a government needed was to have an overly zealous privateer attack a ship from a neutral country—and have that nation turn hostile. Often letters of marque specified people who were not to be molested. One commission, a general instruction to privateers issued by the United States Congress in 1776, read in part:

> You may, by Force of Arms, attack, subdue, and take all Ships and other Vessels belonging to the Inhabitants of Great-Britain, on the High Seas, or between high-water and low-water Marks, except Ships and Vessels bringing Persons who intend to settle and reside in the United Colonies, or bringing Arms, Ammunition or Warlike Stores to the said Colonies . . . which you shall suffer [allow] to pass unmolested. . . .[65]

Documents such as these served two purposes. First, they protected the government by making it quite clear what the pirates were to attack—and what they were to leave alone. Second, they protected the privateer by giving him a legal defense. If captured, the letter of marque enabled him to argue that he was not just a common pirate, but engaged instead in the service of his country. Viewed as a pirate, he would be unceremoniously imprisoned and likely executed; if considered a military prisoner, on the other hand, he would probably earn somewhat better treatment.

The commission, moreover, could also protect a privateer from overzealous civil authorities in his own country. So long as a privateer restricted himself to the terms of the letter of marque, he was free of any punishments for his actions. As an English commission put it, any privateer brought up on piracy charges "shall stand and be freed by vertue of the said Commission."[66]

The exact process by which privateers were hired varied from country to country and time period to time period. As a rule, however, privateers were experienced seamen who had served in important posts in either the country's navy or its merchant fleets. They either had their own ships or were willing to sail one owned by the gov-

Englishman John Hawkins not only had his government's consent to engage in privateering, he was also provided with a ship.

A LETTER OF MARQUE

Privateer Charles de Bils received this letter of marque from the king of Portugal in 1658. The letter is printed in J. Franklin Jameson's Privateering and Piracy in the Colonial Period.

"Know all to whom this my letter patent shall Appeare that itt Behooving mee to provide shipps to oppose sea Roavers thatt frequent the Coasts of these my Kingdomes, for the conveniency of tradeing to them. . . . Itt Is my will and pleasure to nominate and by these Presents doe name [de Bils] for [as] Capt. of a shipp of warr, by virtue of w'ch power hee may provide att his owne charge a shipp of one hundred Tonnes with whatt boates nessesarie, and provide her with Gunns, People, ammunition and provisions as hee shall thinke Convenientt, to wage warr with the subjects of the Kinge of spaine, Turks, Pirats, Sea Roavers, take there shipps and there marchandizes [merchandise] and all that belongs unto them and Carry them to Any Portts of this Kingdome to give An Accountt of them in my office. . . . [H]ee may vizitt or search whatt shippes hee thinks goe loaden with our Enimies goods, goe to there ports, favouringe In all things any Alyed [allied] to this Crowne, Payinge the Customes [that is, custom duties] of sd. [said] Prizes, according to the Rates of the Custome Houses of this Kingdome. Wherefore I Request all Kings, Princes, Potentat[e]s, Lords, Republicks, states, theire Leiftenants [lieutenants], Generalls, Admirals, Governours of there provinces, Citties and Portts, Captaines And Corporals of Warr, to give to the said Charles de Bils all the Assistance, helpe and favour, Passage and Entrance into theire Portts. . . ."

ernment. The Englishman John Hawkins, for example, was given a seven-hundred-ton ship called the *Jesus of Luebeck* by Queen Elizabeth in 1564. Some offered their services to the government, while others were enlisted by its leaders. A few even functioned as mercenaries, offering their services to foreign governments or being recruited by them. In a handful of cases, zealous officials encouraged "their" privateers to sign on for someone else. "When we were at peace," a writer said of a colonial French governor, "he was at the pains of procuring [French privateers'] commissions from Portugal, which country was then at war with Spain. . . ."[67]

Financial Arrangements

Once given their commissions, privateering captains were responsible for outfitting their ships and making them ready for the voyage. This outfitting of ships, of course, represented an enormous cost, far more than most captains could manage on their own. As a result, most privateers had a group of wealthy backers who helped with the initial expenses of supplies, recruitment, and ship maintenance. These men not only brought money to the venture; they also brought prestige. Their number usually included some of the most prominent merchants, courtiers, and financiers of the time and place. Their money made the voyage possible, and their influence served as a further hedge against the possibility of prosecution should the privateer slightly overstep the terms of his commission.

The backers were in it for the glory, but mostly they were in it for the money. So was the captain, and to a lesser extent the crew as well. Exact amounts varied, but the appeal of a privateering voyage was that most of the booty belonged to the backers and the crew. Early in the Golden Age, the English government took 20 percent of all the valuables plundered by the privateers, leaving the captain, crew, and backers to divide up the remainder. Over time the government's share was reduced to 10 percent, and then, in 1708, to nothing at all. The less there was for the government, the more there was for those who participated in privateering. A single voyage could result in enough jewels, gold, silver, and other valuables to make each of the backers and the

captain very rich indeed. Even less valuable prizes were desirable: One ship captured from the British carried "200 Hogsheads [large barrels] of Sugar, a Quantity of Coffee, Indigo, Elephants-Teeth [ivory], Logwood,"[68] and other similar items, but no one was disappointed with the prize.

To be sure, the reverse of this was the possibility of no plunder at all, in which case the privateers and their supporters would lose everything they had invested in the voyage. However, such a result to a privateering expedition was unusual. Indeed, so likely was the possibility of success that some royal governors decided to charge for commissions. Benjamin Fletcher of New York was notorious for doing so, but others requested money as well: one captain gave the governor of Rhode Island five hundred English pounds for his commission in the late seventeenth century, and such stories were common.

Organization

Because of the shares given to the backers and the government, and because the privateering voyages were supported by the government, the structure of a privateering voyage was quite different from a piratical journey. For one thing, privateers often sailed in groups. While some captains, especially during peacetime, sailed alone, there was safety and strength in numbers. In 1744, for example, two Rhode Island privateering ships, the *Revenge* and the *Success*, joined forces. The owners of the ships drew up a contract to seal the agreement, in which they promised that the "Two Sloops or Vessels, Captains, officers, and Companies belonging to them, shall Unite, Assist each other and [act in] Concert together for and during their whole Voyage."[69]

The example of the *Revenge* and the *Success* was not a new idea. A 1708 English privateering voyage to the South Pacific, for example, included two ships—the *Duke* and the *Dutchess* (sometimes spelled *Duchess*)—and a force of over three hundred sailors. The Dutch privateer Piet Heyn easily surpassed this expedition: he once commanded a fleet of thirty-two ships and thirty-five hundred men. While Heyn's flotilla was unusually large by privateering standards, any combining of forces could make the odds of capturing an enemy ship much greater. "There is about 30 privateers now belonging here," read a report from the Caribbean island of Martinique in 1704, "so that it's almost impossible for a vessel to pass to or from the Islands. . . ."[70]

Another difference between pirates and privateers was that privateers did not follow the democratic model of a typical pirate ship. Instead, they organized themselves hierarchically, along the lines of a naval vessel. The captain was fully in charge and rarely let the crew forget that fact. Francis Drake, explained a Spanish nobleman who saw him in action, had complete command of his ship: though he listened to the advice of other officers, he rarely took their recommendations.

English privateers attack a Spanish vessel. Unlike pirates, privateers traveled and attacked in groups.

Even at mealtimes Drake was clearly first among equals. Drake, the nobleman wrote, "is served on silver dishes with gold borders and gilded garlands. . . . He dines and sups to the music of viols."[71]

If the captain had more power, then the crew had correspondingly less. Unlike pirate crews, privateer crews had little say in when to attack, where to journey, and what valuables to take. Many crews, like Drake's, were hired for a set salary. Others were paid a percentage of the loot, the exact amount determined when they signed on. Sometimes the salary system resulted in cries of unfairness, especially when the booty was large. When Heyn's ships returned to the Netherlands, the common seamen rioted upon discovering that they would not share in the plunder.

The privateer captain's success in finding a crew varied considerably. During time of war and of high unemployment, hiring men was easy enough. At other times, it could be more difficult. A few, especially later in the eighteenth century, used newspaper advertisements. "The grand Privateer Ship DEANE, commanded by ELISHA HINMAN, Esq., and prov'd to be a very capital Sailor, will sail on a Cruise against the Enemies of the United States of America,"[72] read a sample ad from a Boston newspaper of 1780. More, however, relied on word of mouth. They spread the word around the docks and in the nearby bars. The better known a captain was and the better his reputation, the easier it was for him to find men willing to work aboard his ship.

A SLIPPERY DEFINITION

Letter of marque or no, the dividing line between pirates and privateers was often hard to find. "The Privateering Stroke so easily degenerates into the Piratical,"[73] mourned the colonial American preacher Cotton Mather in 1704. As the case of Drake indicates, the assignment of a captain to one category or the other frequently depended on who was doing the defining. The Spanish took no comfort in the fact that Drake did not attack English ships or those belonging to English allies: they called him a pirate. The English, in contrast, did take comfort; to them he was a privateer.

Similarly, the rules occasionally changed, especially as European alliances shifted. Privateers had to be careful to keep up with the latest information regarding their nations' friends and enemies. To stay within the letter of the law, for instance, Dutch privateers who brought back booty routinely had to testify that the captains of their Spanish prizes "did not notify us of any peace or truce concluded between the King of Spain and their High Mightinesses [that is, the rulers of the Netherlands]."[74]

Failure to observe the latest alliances put privateers in serious danger of being viewed as pirates. In 1703, for instance, the Englishman John Quelch set out for a voyage aboard a ship called the *Charles*. The purpose of his journey was to attack ships belonging to France and its allies. After plundering several French ships in the North Atlantic, Quelch eventually headed toward Brazil, where his crew overcame a number of ships belonging to

France's ally Portugal. Unfortunately for Quelch, a peace treaty had been signed between Portugal and England before the attack. His commission was no longer valid, and he was hanged for piracy.

Moreover, many men went back and forth between privateering and piracy. Thomas Tew began a privateering career shortly before 1700, when he purchased a part interest in a sloop called the *Amity*. "It was a thing notoriously known to everyone that he had before then been a pirate,"[75] wrote a man who knew him. His background, however, did not stop Tew from obtaining privateering commissions from the governors of Rhode Island, New York, and Bermuda. Tew was assigned to attack French ships and supply bases, and for a

---

A PRIVATEER ATTACKS

This somewhat breathless play-by-play account of an English privateer's attack on a Spanish ship was originally published in 1626. It was written by a Captain John Smith, known as the Admiral of New England, and is quoted by George Francis Dow and John Henry Edmonds in The Pirates of the New England Coast, 1630–1730. *"We are of the sea" was a common pirate or privateer response to the question of where the ship was from.*

"A sail, how stands she, to windward or leeward, set him by the Compass. He stands right a-head. Out with all your sails, a steady man at the helm, sit close to keep her steady. He holds his own. Ho, we gather on him. Out goeth his flag and pennants or streamers, also his Colours, his waist-cloths and top armings, he furls and slings his main sail, in goes his sprit sail and mizzen, he makes ready his close fights fore and after. Well, we shall reach him by and by.

Is all ready? Yes, yes. Every man to his charge. Dowse your top sail, salute him for the sea. Hail him! Whence your ship? Of Spain. Whence is yours? Of England. Are you Merchants or Men of War? We are of the Sea. . . . Give him your stern pieces. Be yare at helm, hail him with a noise of Trumpets.

We are shot through and through, and between wind and water. Try the pump. Master, let us breathe and refresh a little. Sling a man overboard to stop the leak. Done, done. Is all ready again? Yea, yea. Bear up close with him. With all your great and small shot charge him. Board him on his weather quarter. Lash fast your grapplins [grappling hooks, used to pull two ships close together] and shear off, then run stem line the mid ships. Board and board. . . ."

time he did precisely that. Soon, however, Tew and his crew returned to piracy. They attacked wealthy merchant ships belonging to the Arabs, who had no quarrel with England; to the Dutch, who were actually English allies; and finally to the English themselves.

The privateer-to-pirate switch was most obvious following periods of declared war. The fighting created a great need for privateers. The War of the Spanish Succession, for example, lasted from 1702 to 1713 and involved most of the naval powers of western Europe. France, Spain, England, and the Netherlands all engaged experienced captains to serve as privateers. When the war ended and peace was declared, however, the need for privateers dropped considerably. A few stayed on, officially, to continue a low-level form of harassment, but the vast majority of privateers no longer had the support of their respective governments. Some returned to naval or merchant ships, and others found work on land—but a significant number turned to piracy. As a common saying of the period put it, "peace makes pirates."[76]

A few privateers, too, were pirates at heart. Tew was no doubt a good example, but there were many others as well. Though sent out with express instructions to harass an enemy's ships, they nevertheless managed to attack a few "friendly" ships on the way. If the damage done was not too great and the distance from home port far enough, the odds were good that the privateer would never be brought to justice. One early-eighteenth-century crew "insisted that there was never any Privateers Crew hinder'd from Plunder,"[77] regardless of the nation to which the ship belonged, and many other crews agreed.

True, some men reveled in their status as renegade outlaws, especially during the Golden Age. Men such as Blackbeard, Bartholomew Roberts, and Henry Every attacked whomever they pleased, without regard to the interests of their home countries. They soon became as feared and detested by the merchant ships of England as they were by ships from any other nation. These men made it clear that they were in the pirate business to suit themselves, and themselves alone. However, many pirate captains throughout history chose to take a safer path than Blackbeard, Roberts, and Every. They preferred to call themselves privateers, even if they did not always fit the description.

THE EFFECTS OF PRIVATEERING

From a financial standpoint, privateering voyages were often wildly successful. Drake's circumnavigation of the globe is one good example: the booty he took was substantial indeed. There were, however, many others. In 1628 Piet Heyn's enormous fleet captured fifteen Spanish ships in a single raid, taking in almost 5 million silver pesos' worth of coins, metals, cloth, and other valuables. Other raids were nearly as effective, and many backers made enormous amounts of money: earnings of 3,000 percent on an investment were far from rare. "I believe there's more got that way [by privateering] than by turning pirates and robbing,"[78] wrote a colonial governor of New York. To judge by the enthusiasm

An American privateer engages a British ship in combat. During wars, privateers allowed a government to organize a naval force without added costs.

many seamen of the time had for privateering, he was no doubt correct.

But privateering had an effect that went well beyond the question of earning money for their backers. Even unsuccessful voyages, such as that led by the Englishman John Hawkins in 1568, had consequences beneficial to the governments that sponsored the ships. The mere fact that English ships were journeying into hostile Spanish waters was enough to make Spain begin to take England seriously as a sea power. Similarly, the approximately two thousand American ships that served as privateers during the American Revolution did more than simply capture a few British warships:

they served notice to England that the colonies were serious about fighting for their independence. The psychological effect, in each case, was very nearly as important as the actual monetary damages the privateers inflicted.

Some of the effect of privateering involved the military. During wartime, privateering represented an easy and inexpensive way for a small country to add to its naval capacities. Rather than spend millions to purchase, man, and outfit more ships, the government could rely on private citizens to underwrite these costs. Not all privateers were used to attack warships; still, many privateering voyages did capture ports and harass navy fleets in addition to plundering merchant ships. Privateers also found out useful information about coastlines, ports, and oceans that could be passed on to the military. The voyage of the *Duke* and *Dutchess* in 1708 brought English ships to many areas of the globe thirty years in advance of any official naval vessel, but its logbooks and maps were to prove invaluable to later efforts by England to expand its empire.

Outside of declared war, too, privateers had significant political effects. Their movements and their attacks often represented governmental policies and announced the beginning of hostilities between countries. By an edict of the Pope, for example, much of the western Atlantic Ocean belonged to Spain, with the rest the property of Portugal. By sending privateers into this area to plunder and steal, the English made it clear that they did not consider themselves bound by this decision. As an ambassador in the court of Queen Elizabeth I put it, "[The queen] did not understand why either her subjects, or those of any other European Prince, should be debarred from traffic in the Indies."[79] Arguments over who actually owned certain parts of the oceans were often sparked by privateering voyages, and in some cases led to war.

ECONOMIC ISSUES

Privateering had an enormous impact on economics as well. The constant harassment of Spanish vessels by Dutch and English privateers ultimately cost the Spanish government a good deal more than a few treasure-laden ships. In an ef-

fort to ward off the privateers, the Spanish invested heavily in armed escorts for their fleets. If the fleet could bunch together with the guard ships on the outside—not always possible in a time when all ships were operated by sail and oars—the threat of privateer attack was indeed low. But the cost of providing such escorts was enormous. By one estimate, the Spanish spent about 1.4 million silver pesos to protect one treasure fleet in 1632—nearly a third of the total value of the treasure taken by Heyn four years earlier. The treasure arrived safely, but neither the Spanish merchants nor the Spanish rulers could have been happy with the situation.

Even worse where the Spanish were concerned was the fact that much of this money was expressly intended to help wage war—against England, the Netherlands, and other hostile countries. Thus, every gold coin and bar of silver taken by privateers not only weakened the Spanish economy, but also made it more difficult for Spain to pay for a war. In this way, privateers simultaneously had an impact on both economics and politics: the two were tightly connected.

If economic concerns affected political decisions, then the reverse was true as well. One of the central questions in Europe of the sixteenth through eighteenth centuries involved control of trade. With better ships and better maps, European sailors were expanding the range of the known world. New markets and sources of raw materials were appearing every

Turning Pirate After Wartime

The early-twentieth-century pirate historian Philip Gosse, quoted by Jo Stanley in Bold in Her Breeches: Women Pirates Across the Ages, *explained the appeal of piracy in peacetime after a long stretch of privateering during war.*

"When, at the conclusion of hostilities, peace was declared, the crew of a privateer found it exceedingly irksome to give up the roving life and were liable to drift into piracy. Often it happened that, after a long naval war, crews were disbanded, ships laid up, and navies reduced, thus flooding the countryside with idle mariners and filling the roads with begging and starving seamen. These were driven to go to sea if they could find a berth, often half starved and brutally treated, and always underpaid, and so easily yielded to the temptation of joining some vessel bound vaguely for the 'South Sea,' where no questions were asked and no wages paid, but every hand on board had a share in the adventure."

With little to do once a war was over, many privateers turned to a life of piracy during peacetime.

year. Whoever could control trade routes to the Americas, Africa, and Asia had a distinct advantage over the competition. As a result, many European wars of the period, though fought primarily on land and in Europe, were fought for economic dominance as much as for acquisition of territory. By helping their government win the war, privateers could thereby help their countries win control of trade.

6 The End of the Golden Age

For a time in the early part of the eighteenth century, it must have appeared to many merchants that the Golden Age of piracy would continue forever. The strength and spread of the pirates seemed to grow with each passing year, and the various methods used to combat the threat—armed convoys, false gun ports, and the like—were of little avail against the brutality and cleverness of a Blackbeard or a Bartholomew Roberts. But in fact, even while pirate strength was apparently at its greatest, forces were under way that would undermine their power and bring the Golden Age to a quick and sudden end.

TOO MUCH POWER

At its most basic, what happened was simple enough: Merchants and governments decided they were tired of being pushed around by the pirates. This decision was many years in coming. As long as pirates had been arguably privateers—that is, as long as they had restricted themselves to attacking the ships of enemy nations— many politicians had winked at their captures and even their brutalities. Likewise, as long as colonies had benefited from pi-

rates keeping away hostile fleets and adding to the economy, few were quick to condemn piracy.

But even early in the Golden Age, there had been a few voices concerned about the growing influence of pirates. One Pennsylvania official, for example, had complained bitterly about the buccaneers who used his colony as a base, saying:

> They walk the streets with their pockets full of gold, and are the constant companion of the chief in the Government. They threaten my life and those who were active in apprehending them; carry their prohibited goods publicly in boats from one place to another for a market; threaten the lives of the King's collectors and with force and arms rescue the goods from them.[80]

But until the beginning of the eighteenth century, voices such as this man's were few.

Toward the end of the Golden Age, however, nations such as England and the Netherlands increasingly began to realize that the pirates were going too far. The excesses of some of the most violent pirates played a role in this realization. It was hard to defend cruelties such as those inflicted by pirate captain Ned Low, who on at least several occasions sliced off his captives' ears and then forced their owners to eat them. No matter what benefits a Low might offer in terms of protection or increased trade, many officials soon became uncomfortable allowing such men to run free.

More important in the decline of the Golden Age, though, was the increasing tendency of pirates to attack ships of all nations. To help them gain a foothold in the Caribbean, pirates had largely attacked only ships belonging to certain countries. Once established, however, they shifted gears and began to attack anyone who happened by. Plundering an occa-

The increased lawlessness of pirates like Englishman Bartholomew Roberts led to widespread concern on the part of European governments.

sional friendly ship was one thing, but doing so as a matter of routine began to destroy the connections between politicians, merchants, and the buccaneers. Many of the merchants, settlers, and governors on the islands felt betrayed. In 1720, complained a French governor, the English pirate Bartholomew Roberts "seized, burned or sunk fifteen French and English vessels and one Dutch interloper."[81]

The governor no doubt would have preferred Roberts to have limited himself to Spanish ships. But by Roberts's time that was a forlorn hope. Pirates were the dominant power in the West Indies, and increasingly in the mainland American colonies as well. Piracy so frustrated a Cuban governor that it

> occasioned him to swear, in the presence of many, he would never grant quarter to any Pirate that should fall into his hands. But the citizens of Havana desired him not to persist in the execution of that rash and vigorous oath, seeing the Pirates would certainly take occasion thence to do the same; and they [that is, the pirates] had an hundred times more opportunity of revenge than he. . . .[82]

Ultimately, the governor's hands were tied. His power was not nearly as great as that of the lawless buccaneers. Their authority was unmatched by any nation's; they had turned the Caribbean into their own private lake. They were not beholden to the law: they *were* the law. "I am a free prince,"[83] boasted the buccaneer Charles Bellamy, and there were few to contradict him.

TRADE, DIPLOMACY, AND COLONISTS

The main issue with pirates being "free princes," of course, was that pirates were increasingly interfering with the conduct of trade. The prospect of piracy was so great that some merchants gave up trying to send ships through certain areas at all: "British attention focused on the Caribbean in the 1680s and 1720s," writes one historian, "because pirates had succeeded in virtually stopping trade."[84] Without trade, political empires could not continue to grow, merchants would be reduced to ruin, and people accustomed to certain goods would have to learn to do without. By interfering with trade, therefore, pirates were hitting the great nations of Europe where it hurt them the most.

Another issue was that the pirates were drawing European countries into diplomatic crises. The French pirate Raveneau de Lussan stole so much from the Spanish that Spain lodged a formal complaint with France. France, embarrassed, threatened to put de Lussan into prison. As one historian writes, de Lussan had to "bid for a pardon from the authorities for any rupture he might have caused in French-Spanish relations."[85] Similar acts of piracy enraged neutrals and even allies. To keep the peace, it became increasingly necessary for nations to work toward the elimination of the pirates.

Even more serious than pirates who preyed on other European ships were the buccaneers who went after ships from the Indian fleet. The capture of one ship by Henry Every very nearly led to war, as a chronicler of Every's career describes:

ELIMINATING THE PIRATES

In 1704 a proposal to deal with piracy in and around Madagascar was presented in the English Parliament. Much of the stated reason for concern rested on the fact that many of the pirates were English and would bring embarrassment to England if they were allowed to continue. The proposal is quoted in The Pirates *by Douglas Botting.*

"That certain Pyrates having some Years since found the Island of Madagascar to be the most Proper, if not the only Place in the World for their Abode, and carrying on their Destructive Trade with Security, betook themselves thither; and being since increased to a formidable Body are become a manifest Obstruction to Trade, and Scandal to our Nation and Religion, being most of them English, at least four Fifths. . . .

That upon a general Peace, when Multitudes of Soldiers and Seamen will want Employment; or by length of Time, and the Pyrates generating with the Women of the Country [that is, Madagascar], their Numbers should be increased, they may form themselves into a Settlement of Robbers, as Prejudicial to Trade as any on the Coast of Affrica.

For it's natural to consider, That all Persons owe by Instinct a Love to the Place of their Birth: Therefore the present Pyrates must desire to return to their Native Country; and if this present Generation should be once Extinct, their Children will have the same Inclination to Madagascar as these [pirates] have to England, and will not have any such Affection for England, altho' they will retain the Name of English; and consequently all those succeeding Depredations committed by them will be charged to the Account of England. Notwithstanding they were not born with us, so that this seems the only Time for Reducing them to their Obedience, and preventing all those evil Consequences. . . ."

As soon as the news came to the Mogul [emperor], and he knew that they were English who had robbed them, he threatened loud and talked of sending a mighty army with fire and sword to extirpate [wipe out] the English from all their settlements on the Indian coast. The East India Company in England were very much alarmed at it; however, by degrees they found means to pacify him by promising to do their endeavours to take the robbers and deliver them into his hands.[86]

That the pirates were in no way backed by the English government did not matter. The company was able to stave off disaster, but only barely, and the demand for a concerted effort to "extirpate" the pirates grew new life.

The communities of the New World, too, were beginning to grow up. Sugar planters on the West Indian islands were growing rich from the crops they sold, and they increasingly wanted to import goods from elsewhere: fabrics, spices, objects of art. Deliveries of these items, of course, were contingent on the ships that carried them being able to evade or fight off pirates. On a less innocent note, slaves, too, were being imported to the West Indies and coastal North America by planters eager to exploit their labor. Again, pirates threatened the safe arrival of this human cargo; quite often, pirates intercepted the ships that carried slaves and sold them on their own—or enlisted them in their ranks. An early muttering against piracy became a louder grumbling once the colonists realized what pirates were costing them.

Moreover, the New World's colonies were no longer small, insignificant, and in need of all the aid they could get. Instead, they were strong enough to stand alone without help from the pirates—and concerned now with presenting a clean and honest face to the rest of the world. However, becoming known for legitimate trade was difficult as long as pirates sailed in and out of their waters. Officials and merchants in coastal towns, of course, had only themselves to blame: by involving pirates in their political quarrels, they had unleashed a monster that was now threatening their business and their very survival.

HONEST OFFICIALS

By the middle of the Golden Age, therefore, the nations of Europe were increasingly taking a hard line against piracy. Many of the most successful measures they adopted were designed to cut ties between buccaneers and the officials who supported them. In 1695, for example, the king of England decided to replace Benjamin Fletcher as governor of the colony of New York. Fletcher was a notorious pirate sympathizer, and the king wanted someone in office who would not be open to dealings with pirates. "I send you, my

The collaboration between pirates and government officials led to the removal of many colonial governors.

Lord, to New York," the king is quoted as telling his choice, the earl of Bellomont, "because an honest and intrepid man is wanted to put these abuses down, and because I believe you to be such a man."[87] Bellomont was that indeed: among his first actions was sending Fletcher back to London for trial.

Bellomont was not the only honest official to come to power during this time.

Francis Nicholson of Virginia likewise took a strong stand against piracy. In 1700 Nicholson had led a group of sailors in battle against a pirate ship off his colony's coast. Nicholson did not himself fight but provided important moral and economic support. As one witness observed, Nicholson "never stirred off the quarterdeck, but by his example, conduct, and plenty of gold which he gave

AN ACT OF GRACE

In 1717 King George I of England granted an amnesty to most English pirates. Of all Acts of Grace extended to pirates during the Golden Age, this was perhaps the most effective. The text appears in The Pirates of the New England Coast, 1630–1730 *by George Francis Dow and John Henry Edmonds.*

"Whereas we have received information, that several Persons, Subjects of Great Britain, have, since the 24th Day of June, in the Year of our Lord, 1715, committed divers[e] Pyracies and Robberies upon the High-Seas, in the West-Indies, or adjoyning to our Plantations, which hath and may Occasion great Damage to the Merchants of Great Britain, and others trading into those Parts; and tho' we have appointed such a Force as we judge sufficient for suppressing the said Pyrates, yet the more effectually to put an End to the same, we have thought fit, by and with the Advice of our Privy Council, to Issue this our Royal Proclamation; and we do hereby promise, and declare, that in Case any of the said Pyrates, shall on, or before, the 5th of September, in the Year of our Lord 1718, surrender himself or themselves, to one of our Principal Secretaries of State in Great Britain or Ireland, or to any Governor or Deputy Governor of any of our Plantations beyond the Seas; every such Pyrate and Pyrates so surrendering him[self], or themselves, as aforesaid, shall have our gracious Pardon, of, and for such, his or their Pyracy, or Piracies, by him or them committed, before the fifth of January next ensuing. . . ."

amongst the men, made them fight bravely, til they had taken the pirates' ship, with a hundred and odd prisoners, the rest being killed."[88]

Indeed, it soon became a point of honor for some colonials to rid their waters of pirates. In 1718, for instance, Colonel William Rhett of South Carolina determined to capture a pirate named Charles Vane. Reports indicated that Vane was in a cove just to the south of the town of Charleston. As a chronicler of the time wrote, Rhett was "accompanied by many Gentlemen of the Town, animated with the same Principle of Zeal and Honour for our public Safety, and the Preservation of Trade."[89] This was quite a contrast from the South Carolina of even one generation before, when government officials and other "Gentlemen of the Town" had welcomed pirates to Charleston.

Nor did the new officials simply lead expeditions against nearby pirates and make it clear that they themselves were unbribable. Bellomont also came down hard on the merchants who retained ties to the buccaneers. The New York merchant Frederick Philipse, for example, had gotten quite rich off the pirate trade. Bellomont, in response, ordered the coast guard to stop and search several of Philipse's ships. Moreover, Bellomont stripped Philipse of his post on the governor's council. Philipse was furious, and he and some of his fellow businessmen petitioned for Bellomont's removal, but to no avail. By cutting back the colonial market for pirate goods, Bellomont and other governors helped to push the pirates out of business.

AMNESTY AND LAWS

Honest governors were only one prong of the attack on piracy. Another, perhaps equally important, involved the laws. England led the way with an approach that promised rewards for pirates who gave up their way of life. In 1699 the king issued a general amnesty, or Act of Grace, that would apply to virtually all known pirates. Any buccaneer who surrendered his ship and what remained of his booty to English authorities, said the Act of Grace, would escape prosecution for his crimes.

Earlier in the Golden Age, most pirates would probably have ignored such a proposal. But by 1699 times had changed. With officials beginning to crack down on piracy, the number of safe havens for pirates was declining. The odds of capture were going up. Some pirates decided to accept the amnesty, fearing that their luck would soon run out and they would be jailed or executed. Although many pirates still opted to take their chances, the English government nevertheless considered the 1699 Act of Grace a success.

Indeed, it worked well enough that similar amnesties would be extended over the the next few years—whenever the numbers of pirates seemed to be getting high. Sometimes the amnesty covered all pirates operating in a certain area. An Act of Grace might apply to all pirates in the Indian and Pacific Oceans, for example, if that was where the greatest problems lay. Similarly, local governors sometimes proclaimed amnesties of their own. Woodes Rogers, governor of the Bahamas, granted amnesty to over six hundred buccaneers who cruised in the waters near his jurisdiction.

Extending amnesty was a tricky business, however. It was important not to do it so often that would-be pirates would come to expect it—thereby marauding all they pleased in hopes of a pardon soon afterward. On the other hand, for the Acts of Grace to work effectively, it was necessary to offer them as soon as they might actually dissuade pirates from continuing. Typically, government officials offered amnesty with clearly defined deadlines and specified means of surrender. The terms of an Act of Grace from 1717, for example, explained in part that

> we [that is, the king] do hereby promise, and declare, that in Case any of the said Pyrates [in and around the Bahamas], shall on, or before, the 5th of September, in the Year of our Lord 1718, surrender him or themselves, to one of our Principal Secretaries of State in Great Britain or Ireland . . . [then] every such Pyrate and Pyrates so surrendering him, or themselves, as aforesaid, shall have our gracious Pardon . . . .[90]

At the same time as governments offered pardons to those who turned themselves in of their own free will, they also made legal changes designed to make prosecutions easier and guilty verdicts more likely. England, for instance, set up new courts strictly for trying pirates. Earlier, at the beginning of the Golden Age, pirates were supposed to be sent to England for trial, but few were. The time and cost involved were both great, and corrupt colonial governors often arranged for "trials" never reported to England and rigged to result in a not-guilty verdict.

These new courts—so-called vice-admiralty courts—helped put a stop to that practice. They enabled governments to have pirates stand trial nearly anywhere in English territory—mother country and colony alike. Governor Nicholson of Virginia was permitted, for example, to hold "Tryall of Pyrates in Virga. [Virginia] or Carolina or at Sea."[91] The vice-admiralty courts were staffed by government and naval personnel, along with men appointed directly by the king—no longer did colonial governors run the show. The courts were equipped to push cases through quickly and honestly, and the result was predictable: a sudden upsurge in the number of pirates found guilty and brought to justice.

Another law also proved highly effective in limiting piracy. This was an act of Parliament, passed in 1721, which made trafficking with pirates a crime equivalent to piracy itself. Since piracy was a capital offense, this meant that anyone who bought goods from the buccaneers, sold them supplies, or gave them any other kind of aid was in danger of execution. The stakes were too high, and many people who had previously supported the pirates no longer were willing to do so.

Policing the Seas

But honest officials, amnesties, and tougher laws were all useless without a concerted

New laws and new courts guaranteed that pirates would be brought to justice.

effort to police the oceans and capture the pirates. For many years this had not happened; the seas had been left to the pirates, stopped only occasionally by the weak efforts of the merchants themselves. The constant round of wars in Europe diverted the attention of most navies. Worse, frequent sea battles cost ships, equipment, and lives, weakening the fleets if they should decide to go after the pirates. Moreover, the opinion of many national leaders was that the pirates were too powerful to overcome anyway. Well into the 1690s, for instance, England refused repeated requests by the East India Company to send the Royal Navy to patrol the Indian Ocean. Much of the reason was the perceived need to keep the fleet at home in case of possible attack by the French.

But the problem of piracy proved too serious to ignore, and by the turn of the century, ideas were changing. First, governors such as Lord Bellomont began to send out special privateers—men who were supposed to prey upon the pirates themselves rather than on the ships flying a certain enemy flag. This represented a major step: Sending a privateer to attack the pirates was a recognition that piracy had become every bit as dangerous to a power as any other enemy nation. Like all privateering voyages, these trips were official but did not involve any of the resources of the country and its navy.

However, privateering voyages did not work out precisely as planned. The best known of these privateering captains was William Kidd, and his story points out some of the flaws with the privateering system. In 1695 Kidd was assigned to capture a long list of individual pirates

and other subjects, natives or inhabitants of New York, and elsewhere in our Plantations in America, [who] have associated themselves, with divers[e] others, wicked and ill-disposed persons, and do, against the Law of Nations, commit many and great Piracies, robberies and depredations on the seas upon the parts of America . . . to the great hindrance and discouragement of trade and navigation.[92]

One problem Kidd faced was with the nature of piracy itself. By the letter of the law, privateers could not attack ships except those from nations listed specifically on their letters of marque. That was all very well for ships of recognized nations, which typically flew their own national colors, as the custom of the sea required. Pirate ships, on the other hand, had a disconcerting tendency to fly flags of whatever nations they chose. Kidd was forced to leave a vessel alone if it flew a Dutch or Danish flag, for example, even if the ship looked like a pirate craft in all other ways.

Moreover, Kidd would earn his money in the same way as other privateers typically did: by taking booty from the ships he raided. Again, that was acceptable for traditional privateers, who preyed on merchant ships heavily laden with valuable goods. In theory, pirate ships would be just as rich a prize, but in practice they rarely were. The privateers' share was dependent on what the pirates had taken, and not all pirate ships had managed to capture much booty. Moreover, even when buccaneers did make major captures, they sometimes headed directly to a friendly port and spent their gains rather than continuing to sail with the treasure on board.

Kidd pointed out the flaws in the system, but his superiors brushed aside his concerns. Later Kidd would say he had been forced to accept the assignment. Certainly he was saddled with terms that put him at great financial and personal risk if the trip was less than a smashing success. After having been arrested for attacking several decidedly nonpirate ships, Kidd

After being captured, Captain William Kidd was found guilty of piracy and hanged.

complained that he had been given permission to do so by his superiors, should the pirate hunt prove less profitable than he wished. "Lord Bellomont assured me again and again," he wrote, "that the noble lords would stifle all complaints."[93] His pleas were to no avail: Kidd was found guilty of piracy and hanged.

THE ROYAL NAVY

Soon after the Captain Kidd debacle, however, England gave up on privateering expeditions. Instead, the English government altered its long-standing policy and began to make use of official naval ships to police the oceans and eradicate the pirates. The decision to do this was controversial. King William himself worried that attacking pirates would seriously weaken English defenses against France, the latest enemy of England. But the Tory political party in Parliament insisted. The pirates were a greater danger than France, they argued, and their view carried the day.

As a result of the Tories' doggedness, England sent out several ships to patrol the oceans every year between 1699 and the end of the Golden Age some twenty or thirty years later. Individually, none of these warships had any obvious effect on the number of pirates. There were few great captures of whole fleets of pirate ships, few raids against pirate settlements that resulted in the wholesale capture of hundreds of buccaneers. The expeditions that ultimately resulted in the capture of some of the greatest pirate captains—Blackbeard, Bartholomew Roberts, and others—usually required weeks, even months, of persistent sailing; defeating a Blackbeard was hardly the sort of thing a warship did every couple of days or so.

But the ships, taken collectively, did have an effect. The first great naval attack on piracy, led by Commodore Thomas Warren, cruised the Indian Ocean in 1699. Warren caught not a single ship and fired not a single shot on coastal settlements. Still, his voyage was a clear success. Warren sailed off the Madagascar shore, demonstrating the power of his guns and spreading the word about the latest offer of amnesty. Fearing for their lives, many pirates—over half of those on Madagascar at the time, according to one estimate—decided to accept the Act of Grace. The others abandoned their towns, their ships, and their plunder and headed for the interior of the island.

Other expeditions had similar results. Woodes Rogers brought four small warships with him when he assumed the governorship of the Bahamas in 1718. The naval vessels spent most of their time lying peacefully in the harbor, but they served notice to pirates that Rogers meant business, and Blackbeard, Charles Vane, and other pirates gave the Bahamas a wide berth. In Blackbeard's case, moreover, the presence of the warships pushed him closer to Virginia, where he was ultimately defeated—by two other warships under the command of English naval officers.

Gradually, the noose tightened. Pirates had little trouble attacking a merchant ship, but a naval vessel was something else again. Wherever pirates roamed, warships sooner or later arrived; and the sight alone was usually enough to scatter them. In every case, some gave up piracy, accepting pardons or moving into more legitimate lines of work. The rest found that they had less and less ocean to work with—and, of course, a less helpful citizenry on the shores.

Worse yet for the pirates, many of the most famous and successful buccaneer captains were being captured. Blackbeard fell in 1718, Calico Jack Rackham in 1721, Bartholomew Roberts a year later. Each was the victim of naval vessels, warships that had steadily tracked their movements and then gone in for the kill. Lesser pirates could not help but fear for their own lives.

MODERN-DAY PIRATES

Piracy continues even in the present, especially in the oceans around less-developed countries. Their crimes are similar, but their looks are different, as Jo Stanley explains in her book Bold in Her Breeches.

"Far from being dressed today in picturesque brocade jackets and feathered tricorn hats, male pirates today are reported as wearing anything from loincloths to ragged jogging suits, black bandanas, US Army surplus combat uniforms, and . . . plastic flip-flops. Pirates who robbed the Danish *Arktis Sun* in the Persian Gulf in February 1990 wore black robes and red Arab scarves. . . .

Some of the items reported stolen reveal the extent of pirates' poverty and desperation: Ovaltine, clothes, the side window of a [truck], . . . ship's cutlery, a few fathoms of polypropylene rope. Others choose resaleable goods such as drugs, electrical ware, cigarettes, pharmaceuticals, food, computers or gas lighters. Reports of losses range from cocoa butter in the Canary Islands . . . to cement in Apapa and handbags in Lome. Some of the stolen goods are taken from the ship as travelling warehouse, but others are taken from the ship as home, and as small floating office. Pirates often steal the crew's personal property— videotapes and credit cards, television and binoculars. The best booty is cash: heists have been as high as $1,000, twice the average annual income of a waged Indonesian. Many pirates know that the captains keep the safe keys in desk drawers or on the bookshelf. . . . The captain's cabin can also yield malt whisky, his Seiko watch and wallet."

The balance of power had shifted, and the pirates who remained had to wonder whether continuing to plunder made any sense.

Things had changed. Once, pirate captains had been the heroes, the king of the roost, the men who held the power and made millions tremble. Once, pirate crews had had the support of the great men of the colonies. Now, pirates were taking amnesty and being unceremoniously hanged if they did not, assuming they were lucky enough to avoid being shot to death during sea battles they could not win. Now, the captains who caught the pirates became the heroes. Chaloner Ogle, who killed Roberts, was knighted for his actions.

Piracy did not end by any means in 1720 or 1730. Privateering continued, of course, through the American Revolution and into the War of 1812. Piracy on the Mediterranean's Barbary Coast continued well into the nineteenth century. In the China Sea, pirates fought government authorities to standoffs in the middle of the 1800s, and continued to disrupt trade during the early part of the twentieth century as well. In some parts of the world—notably southeast Asia—piracy continues today. But never again would pirates have the power, the respect, the wealth, or the sheer numbers that they had enjoyed between 1650 and 1730. When the Golden Age came to an end, the pirates' place in the making of history was over for good.

7 Legacies of the Golden Age

The events of piracy's Golden Age had an enormous effect on the course of history. Some of these effects came about as a direct result of the pirates themselves. It is entirely fair to say, for example, that pirates helped open up the world. While buccaneers rarely roamed far outside shipping routes, their voyages led to greater geographical and anthropological understanding. Few pirates kept journals, but some did—and others, especially those who claimed that they were really privateers, wrote down their reminiscences years after their voyages were over.

These works are filled with information about the world as it appeared in the seventeenth and early eighteenth centuries. Often their reports added to the world's knowledge of coastlines, harbors, prevailing winds, and islands far from Europe. Often, too, they wrote detailed descriptions of the people they found. Exaggeration and misunderstanding was common in these reports; still, the experiences of pirates increased general knowledge about the world.

But pirates changed the world in much more significant ways than simply adding geographic knowledge and extending Europeans' understanding of other peoples.

Pirates had an especially large effect on the politics and government of early modern Europe. Both their predations and the attempts made by nations to stifle them changed the course of European history forever. Moreover, the reality of piracy forced nations to alter their way of thinking when it came to questions of commerce, governance, and even nationhood itself.

POLITICAL CHANGE

Perhaps the most obvious legacies of piracy involved political changes—and most obvious of those, in turn, was piracy's effect on the Spanish Empire. In the early 1500s, Spain had been the greatest naval power in Europe; no other nation came close. Spain's colonial holdings were vast—and had the potential for making Spain far wealthier than it already was. When ships began to carry gold, silver, and jewels home to Madrid, it seemed improbable that Spain would ever take second place to any other nation.

But in great part because of pirates, Spanish power slowly declined over the next few centuries. First came the Dutch,

French, and English privateers, who attacked ship after ship and prevented a significant chunk of Spanish treasure from ever reaching the safety of the royal vaults. Next came the buccaneers themselves, who diverted Spanish loot not into national treasuries but into their own pockets. Spanish officials did what they could to stop the pirates, but the defensive measures they took were both costly and generally ineffective. No matter how many small ships were outfitted to protect merchant fleets against the pirates, trade was still cut back for years, with a resulting loss of income to merchants and governments alike. As one historian writes:

> The pirates may not [always] have reaped the treasures they were after, but they certainly sowed their share of fear; direct hits like Piet Heyn's or Henry Morgan's were rare, but indirect losses in unused armaments, soldiers' salaries, and unnecessary fortifications grew to be substantial, if not staggering. Exactly how costly they were cannot be known with precision, but Spain and its colonies would most certainly have been happier and more prosperous without them.[94]

Of course, piracy was not responsible for all the Spanish decline. The victory of the English fleet against the Spanish Armada in 1588 was accomplished with little, if any, help from pirates. Spain's holdings in the New World were probably too large to police successfully; even if pirates had not raided coastal settlements and attacked treasure ships, it is likely that other nations would eventually have established footholds inside Spanish areas. And the treasure Spain did manage to bring back home was not always spent with the best interests of the nation in mind. Nevertheless, the privateers and buccaneers who siphoned off millions of dollars' worth of valuables from Spanish ships and settlements certainly played an important role in the decline of the Spanish Empire.

The Golden Age had another important political effect as well. The cozy connections early on between the pirates and the American colonists were not always acceptable to the English who governed the colonies. For many years the colonists more or less openly helped the pirates, while English merchants and government

Pirate attacks during the Golden Age affected not only trade, but also politics among various nations.

CAPTAIN KIDD

"My name was Robert Kidd, when I sail'd, when I sail'd,
My name was Robert Kidd, when I sail'd.
My name was Robert Kidd, God's law I did forbid,
And so wickedly I did, when I sail'd.

I'd a Bible in my hand, when I sail'd, when I sail'd,
I'd a Bible in my hand, when I sail'd.
I'd a Bible in my hand, by my father's great command,
But I sunk it in the sand, when I sail'd.

I murdered William Moore, as I sail'd, as I sail'd,
I murdered William Moore, as I sail'd.
I murdered William Moore, and left him in his gore,
Not many leagues from shore, as I sail'd.

I'd ninety bars of gold, as I sail'd, as I sail'd,
I'd ninety bars of gold, as I sail'd.
I'd ninety bars of gold, and dollars manifold,
With riches uncontrolled, as I sail'd.

Come all ye young and old, see me die, see me die,
Come all ye young and old, see me die.
Come all ye young and old, you're welcome to my gold,
For by it I've lost my soul, and must die."

officials fumed. The difference of approach helped establish that the colonies' interests were not always the same as British interests. The perspective on pirates was only one of many divisions that would crop up between colonists and those in the mother country, but it was a major one. In the long run, divisions such as these would help pave the way for the American Revolution.

COMMERCE AND THE NATIONAL INTEREST

Piracy was extremely destructive to the Spanish, and it could easily have proved so for all nations. Early in the Golden Age, England had been content to allow the East India Company and other mercantile concerns to fight off pirates as best they could. They were private companies, the government reasoned, and thus the national interest was not at stake; moreover, naval fleets had other, more pressing responsibilities. This perspective was sensible enough, but it ignored one important fact: the companies, by themselves, could not ward off the buccaneers. Had England continued with this policy, it is likely that the merchants would have been damaged, even forced into bankruptcy, and trade in and out of Great Britain would have been seriously compromised. Without trade, in turn, England might never have become a great sea power.

But in fact nothing of the sort happened. As the Golden Age progressed, it became increasingly apparent to England—and to the Netherlands and France as well—that state support of commerce was a good investment: it helped make a country important and influential, and it helped keep it that way. Laws proclaiming amnesties and stiffening penalties against pirates were part of the equation, but sending out naval vessels in search of buccaneers was perhaps even more important. The threat of piracy helped establish the notion that a great country had an interest in promoting sea trade. "Sea commerce," writes a researcher, "was seen as fundamental to national power."[95]

The outbreak of piracy during the Golden Age also led to surprising international cooperation. When pirates threatened to overcome ships of all nations, nations increasingly banded together to stop them. Former enemies sent out ships to capture raiders that harassed them both. Christians and Muslims, bitter enemies for

centuries, together agreed that the buccaneers had to be removed. The war on piracy helped bring the world closer together. More than that, it helped pave the way for international agreements among countries, laws that would protect and regulate commerce of all nations and make another pirate outbreak more difficult. The pirate hunters of the early eighteenth century had no intention of establishing a plan of international unity when they helped one another attack the last remaining pirates; but in the long run, that was exactly what they did.

The Golden Age also sparked a new way of thinking among Europeans. For years crime had been seen as inevitable. On the sea there were pirates, on land highwaymen and robbers. Moving cargo meant absorbing losses, and all merchants expected and accepted it. The alternative was an expensive system of patrols and guards that threatened to eat up profits and still might not be successful. The sheer number of pirates during the Golden Age, however, helped change the view of crime as a given.

The enormous losses to piracy, as one observer writes, made the English and their colonists "put behind them the idea that they could afford crime better than they could afford an adequate police force."[96] Of course, the change in thinking was far from immediate, nor was it accepted by all; for years to come, merchants and governments would scrimp on police forces and write off losses to crime as part of the cost of doing business. Still, one outcome of the Golden Age was an increasing sense that crime was not inevitable, that it could—and should—be stopped.

PIRATES IN POPULAR CULTURE

Today perhaps the greatest impact of pirates is on popular culture. Beginning shortly after the end of the Golden Age, pirates became a widespread fascination—a fascination that continues well into the present time. The paintings of Howard Pyle, an illustrator of the late nineteenth century, are an excellent example. Pyle's pictures show pirates in action—boarding a treasure ship, taking prisoners, marooning a colleague.

GILBERT AND SULLIVAN'S PIRATE KING

The team of playwright William S. Gilbert and composer Arthur Sullivan wrote fourteen comic operettas at the end of the nineteenth century. Among the most popular of these works was The Pirates of Penzance, *which focused on a band of overly sentimental pirates who refused to attack orphans. In the Pirate King's song "Oh, Better Far to Live and Die," Gilbert used the pirates to satirize the business and government leaders of the time. The text is quoted in Ian Bradley's* The Complete Annotated Gilbert and Sullivan.

Actor Kevin Kline in a scene from The Pirates of Penzance.

"Oh, better far to live and die
Under the brave black flag I fly,
Than play a sanctimonious part,
With a pirate head and a pirate heart.
Away to the cheating world go you,
Where pirates all are well-to-do;
But I'll be true to the song I sing,
And live and die a Pirate King. . . .

When I sally forth to meet my prey,
I help myself in a royal way:
I sink a few more ships, it's true,
Then a well-bred monarch ought to do;
But many a king on a first-class throne,
If he wants to call his crown his own,
Must manage somehow to get through
More dirty work than ever *I* do. . . ."

Pyle's pictures were enormously popular during his time, and they have remained so through the years since they were first produced; many books about pirates reproduce at least a few of his paintings.

Pirates have had an impact over the years on drama and literature as well. Robert Louis Stevenson's novel *Treasure Island* is one of many stories dealing with pirates. The English team of playwright W. S. Gilbert and composer Arthur Sullivan's operetta *The Pirates of Penzance*, written during the 1870s, is still frequently performed today—and has appeared in several updated versions as well. And nearly everyone knows the character of Captain Hook and his band of pirates in the book, movie, or stage musical versions of *Peter Pan*.

However, none of these portrayals of pirates relies especially heavily on the historical record. There is no record, for instance, of pirates ever making a prisoner walk the plank, but one of Pyle's most famous works shows exactly that. In real life, likewise, pirates seldom if ever buried their treasure, as Stevenson had them doing in *Treasure Island*; they were much more interested in spending their booty. Similarly, the buccaneers in *The Pirates of Penzance* are far from accurately drawn: Gilbert's creations are too tenderhearted to make piracy pay.

But the pirates in these and other works of popular culture were not intended to be historically accurate. They speak, instead, to the needs and circumstances of our own society—and the times during which these works were created. Modern civilization has brought many benefits to the Western world, but the fascination with pirates suggests that perhaps something has been lost: at heart, pirates represent the complete opposite of today's safe and predictable world.

In the popular imagination, the pirate's life is one of adventure and drama. Moreover, pirates stand for a wild sort of freedom. Pirates did what they wanted and thumbed their noses at the rules of polite society. Pirates are intriguing subjects for movies, books, and art because the life of a pirate seems so much at odds with normal everyday life today. From children in school to carpenters and accountants on the job, the regimented and ordered life of modern times can seem overwhelmingly dull, overwhelmingly trite, and overwhelmingly structured.

At a distance of several centuries, it is easy to overlook the brutalities, the hardships, and the evils of pirate life in favor of the romance, the adventure, and the freedom. Perhaps it is no wonder that for well over a hundred years, Westerners have eagerly sought refuge from the realities of modern life in material dealing with pirates.

Notes

Introduction: Piracy in Early Times

1. Quoted in Henry A. Ormerod, *Piracy in the Ancient World*. Liverpool: University Press of Liverpool, 1924, p. 68.

2. Quoted in Jo Stanley, ed., *Bold in Her Breeches: Women Pirates Across the Ages*. London: Harper-Collins, 1995, p. 29.

3. Stanley, *Bold in Her Breeches*, p. 24.

Chapter 1: Development of the Golden Age

4. Quoted in C. H. Haring, *The Buccaneers in the West Indies in the XVII Century*. New York: E. P. Dutton, 1910, p. 31.

5. Haring, *The Buccaneers in the West Indies*, p. 38.

6. Quoted in Hamilton Cochran, *Pirates of the Spanish Main*. New York: American Heritage Publishing, 1961, p. 41.

7. George Francis Dow and John Henry Edmonds, *The Pirates of the New England Coast, 1630–1730*. Salem, MA: Marine Research Society, 1923, p. 10.

8. James Burney, *History of the Buccaneers of America*. London: Unit Library, 1902, pp. 45–46.

9. Quoted in Hugh Rankin, *The Golden Age of Piracy*. Williamsburg, VA: Colonial Williamsburg, 1969, p. 5.

10. Quoted in Dow and Edmonds, *Pirates of the New England Coast*, p. 12.

11. Quoted in Cochran, *Pirates of the Spanish Main*, p. 54.

12. Quoted in Douglas Botting, *The Pirates*. Alexandria, VA: Time-Life Books, 1978, p. 138.

13. Quoted in Botting, *The Pirates*, p. 73.

14. Quoted in Kris E. Lane, *Pillaging the Empire*. Armonk, NY: M. E. Sharpe, 1998, p. 135.

15. Quoted in Dow and Edmonds, *Pirates of the New England Coast*, p. 96.

Chapter 2: Lives of the Pirates

16. Quoted in Emily Morison Beck, ed., *Bartlett's Familiar Quotations*. 15th ed. Boston: Little, Brown, 1980, p. 264.

17. Quoted in Rankin, *The Golden Age of Piracy*, p. 29.

18. Alexander Exquemelin, *The Buccaneers of America*. London: Swan Sonnenschein and Company, 1893, p. 60.

19. Quoted in Rankin, *The Golden Age of Piracy*, p. 29.

20. Quoted in Botting, *The Pirates*, p. 47.

21. Quoted in Dow and Edmonds, *Pirates of the New England Coast*, p. 353.

22. Quoted in Botting, *The Pirates*, p. 50.

23. Quoted in Botting, *The Pirates*, p. 51.

24. Quoted in Robert Carse, *The Age of Piracy*. New York: Rinehart and Company, 1957, p. 7.

25. Quoted in Rankin, *The Golden Age of Piracy*, p. 31.

26. Quoted in Botting, *The Pirates*, p. 51.

27. Quoted in Lane, *Pillaging the Empire*, p. 130.

28. Quoted in Fleming MacLiesh and Martin L. Krieger, *The Privateers: A Raiding Voyage to the Great South Sea*. New York: Random House, 1962, p. 19.

29. Quoted in Botting, *The Pirates*, p. 51.

30. Quoted in Botting, *The Pirates*, p. 46.

31. Exquemelin, *The Buccaneers of America*, p. 423.

32. Quoted in Lane, *Pillaging the Empire*, p. 194.

33. Quoted in Stanley, *Bold in Her Breeches*, p. 166.

34. Quoted in Peter Kemp Kemp, *Brethren of the Coast*. New York: St. Martin's Press, 1961, p. 98.

Chapter 3: Pirates and the World Around Them

35. Quoted in Rankin, *The Golden Age of Piracy*, p. 40.

36. Quoted in J. Franklin Jameson, *Privateering and Piracy in the Colonial Period*. New York: Macmillan, 1923, p. 102.

37. Quoted in Rankin, *The Golden Age of Piracy*, p. 111.

38. Quoted in Jameson, *Privateering and Piracy in the Colonial Period*, p. 150.

39. Quoted in Botting, *The Pirates*, p. 31.

40. Quoted in Rankin, *The Golden Age of Piracy*, p. 91.

41. Rankin, *The Golden Age of Piracy*, p. 33.

42. Quoted in Rankin, *The Golden Age of Piracy*, p. 23.

43. Quoted in Rankin, *The Golden Age of Piracy*, p. 12.

44. Lane, *Pillaging the Empire*, p. 105.

45. Quoted in Dow and Edmonds, *Pirates of the New England Coast*, p. 12.

46. Dow and Edmonds, *Pirates of the New England Coast*, p. 349.

47. Quoted in Rankin, *The Golden Age of Piracy*, p. 82.

48. Haring, *The Buccaneers in the West Indies*, p. 251.

49. Stanley, *Bold in Her Breeches*, p. 31.

50. Rudyard Kipling, *Puck of Pook's Hill*. Garden City, NY: Doubleday, 1905, p. 206.

Chapter 4: Pirates and Their Victims

51. Quoted in Botting, *The Pirates*, p. 90.

52. Quoted in Botting, *The Pirates*, p. 68.

53. Stanley, *Bold in Her Breeches*, p. 153.

54. Frank Sherry, *Raiders and Rebels: The Golden Age of Piracy*. New York: William Morrow, 1986, p. 376.

55. Botting, *The Pirates*, p. 138.

56. Quoted in Botting, *The Pirates*, p. 62.

57. Quoted in Rankin, *The Golden Age of Piracy*, p. 147.

58. Exquemelin, *The Buccaneers of America*, p. 229.

59. Lane, *Pillaging the Empire*, p. 136.

60. Quoted in Botting, *The Pirates*, p. 17.

61. Quoted in Eric Partridge, *Pirates, Highwaymen, and Adventurers*. London: Scholartis Press, 1927, p. 137.

62. Botting, *The Pirates*, p. 55.

Chapter 5: Pirates and Privateers

63. Quoted in Haring, *The Buccaneers in the West Indies*, p. 41.

64. Quoted in Jameson, *Privateering and Piracy in the Colonial Period*, p. 27.

65. Quoted in C. Keith Wilbur, *Pirates and Patriots of the Revolution*. Old Saybrook, CT: Globe Pequot Press, 1973, p. 26.

66. Quoted in Jameson, *Privateering and Piracy in the Colonial Period*, p. 351.

67. Quoted in Burney, *History of the Buccaneers of America*, pp. 47–48.

68. Quoted in Jameson, *Privateering and Piracy in the Colonial Period*, p. 572.

69. Quoted in Jameson, *Privateering and Piracy in the Colonial Period*, p. 463.

70. Quoted in Jameson, *Privateering and Piracy in the Colonial Period*, p. 277.

71. Quoted in Lane, *Pillaging the Empire*, p. 47.

72. Quoted in Wilbur, *Pirates and Patriots of the Revolution*, p. 29.

73. Quoted in Dow and Edmonds, *Pirates of the New England Coast*, p. 10.

74. Quoted in Jameson, *Privateering and Piracy in the Colonial Period*, p. 13.

75. Quoted in Dow and Edmonds, *Pirates of the New England Coast*, p. 84.

76. Quoted in Dow and Edmonds, *Pirates of the New England Coast*, p. xix.

77. Quoted in MacLiesh and Krieger, *The Privateers*, p. 31.

78. Quoted in Dow and Edmonds, *Pirates of the New England Coast*, p. 19.

79. Quoted in Burney, *History of the Buccaneers of America*, p. 32.

Chapter 6: The End of the Golden Age

80. Quoted in Botting, *The Pirates*, p. 27.

81. Quoted in Botting, *The Pirates*, p. 166.

82. Quoted in Exquemelin, *The Buccaneers of America*, p. 83.

83. Quoted in Rankin, *The Golden Age of Piracy*, p. 25.

84. Quoted in Stanley, *Bold in Her Breeches*, p. 32.

85. Carse, *The Age of Piracy*, p. 178.

86. Quoted in Partridge, *Pirates, Highwaymen, and Adventurers*, p. 116.

87. Quoted in Sherry, *Raiders and Rebels*, p. 148.

88. Quoted in Sherry, *Raiders and Rebels*, p. 198.

89. Quoted in Rankin, *The Golden Age of Piracy*, p. 97.

90. Quoted in Dow and Edmonds, *Pirates of the New England Coast*, p. 381.

91. Quoted in Rankin, *The Golden Age of Piracy*, p. 78.

92. Quoted in Cochran, *Pirates of the Spanish Main*, p. 98.

93. Quoted in Sherry, *Raiders and Rebels*, p. 160.

Chapter 7: Legacies of the Golden Age

94. Lane, *Pillaging the Empire*, p. 202.

95. Sherry, *Raiders and Rebels*, p. 365.

96. Rankin, *The Golden Age of Piracy*, p. 158.

For Further Reading

Robert Carse, *The Age of Piracy.* New York: Rinehart and Company, 1957. A somewhat novelistic account of the Golden Age. Thorough and detailed.

Hamilton Cochran, *Pirates of the Spanish Main.* New York: American Heritage Publishing, 1961. Intended for young adults, this book is a thorough look at the English privateers of the sixteenth century and the events of the Golden Age. Particular emphasis on the personalities who went pirating; exceptionally well illustrated.

Stuart Kallen, *Life Among the Pirates.* San Diego: Lucent Books, 1999. A thorough and carefully written description of life aboard a pirate ship, with some information about the development of piracy and the end of the Golden Age.

Peter Kemp Kemp, *Brethren of the Coast.* New York: St. Martin's Press, 1961. Focuses on piracy in the South Pacific and Indian Oceans.

C. Keith Wilbur, *Pirates and Patriots of the Revolution.* Old Saybrook, CT: Globe Pequot Press, 1973. The typefaces can make this book very difficult to read, but this is an excellent encyclopedia-style account of the colonial privateers who helped win the American Revolution. Full of diagrams and drawings.

Works Consulted

Douglas Botting, *The Pirates*. Alexandria, VA: Time-Life Books, 1978. An excellent account of piracy with particular focus on the Golden Age, this book also discusses the world that surrounded piracy. Well illustrated and informative about the lives of various pirate captains.

Ian Bradley, *The Complete Annotated Gilbert and Sullivan*. Oxford: Oxford University Press, 1986. Librettos of British operettas written by lyricist W. S. Gilbert and composer Arthur Sullivan, including their parody of piracy, *The Pirates of Penzance*.

James Burney, *History of the Buccaneers of America*. London: Unit Library, 1902. Dated in its language and attitudes but nevertheless useful for its frequent quotations from primary source accounts of piracy.

David Cordingly, *Under the Black Flag: The Romance and Reality of Life Among the Pirates*. New York: Harcourt, Brace, 1997. Focuses on the details of life on board pirate ships, but also includes information on the world around pirates as well.

George Francis Dow and John Henry Edmonds, *The Pirates of the New England Coast, 1630–1730*. Salem, MA: Marine Research Society, 1923. A long account of the pirates and privateers who used New England as a home base or cruised off its shores in search of prey.

Good information on the connections between the pirates and those onshore.

Alexander Exquemelin, *The Buccaneers of America*. London: Swan Sonnenschein and Company, 1893. Alexander Exquemelin, or Esquemeling, was a pirate; this book includes his narrative of how he became a pirate and what he did as one, in addition to including other first-person accounts of piracy.

C. H. Haring, *The Buccaneers in the West Indies in the XVII Century*. New York: E. P. Dutton, 1910. More focused on privateering expeditions than on piracy itself, and particularly useful for describing the events that led up to the Golden Age. The author, though an Englishman, comes across as surprisingly sympathetic to the Spanish perspective.

J. Franklin Jameson, *Privateering and Piracy in the Colonial Period*. New York: Macmillan, 1923. A fascinating book of documents relating to piracy off the North American coast. Included are letters of marque, depositions of those caught by pirates, letters regarding pirates, and much more.

Rudyard Kipling, *Puck of Pook's Hill*. Garden City, NY: Doubleday, 1905. A children's book popular in the early twentieth century; includes Kipling's poem "A Smuggler's Song."

Kris E. Lane, *Pillaging the Empire*. Armonk, NY: M. E. Sharpe, 1998. A thorough and thoughtful analysis of the effect of piracy on the New World, most specifically in Latin America. Lane especially investigates the role that pirates and privateers played in the downfall of the Spanish Empire.

Fleming MacLiesh and Martin L. Krieger, *The Privateers: A Raiding Voyage to the Great South Sea*. New York: Random House, 1962. A detailed account of the 1708 journey of two English privateering vessels, the *Duke* and the *Dutchess*, to Spanish territory in the South Pacific.

Henry A. Ormerod, *Piracy in the Ancient World*. Liverpool: University Press of Liverpool, 1924. A study of the pirates who cruised the Mediterranean Sea in Greek and Roman times.

Eric Partridge, *Pirates, Highwaymen, and Adventurers*. London: Scholartis Press, 1927. A collection of extracts from books dealing with robbery through history. Some are fictional, others taken from real life.

Hugh Rankin, *The Golden Age of Piracy*. Williamsburg, VA: Colonial Williamsburg, 1969. A well-written account of the Golden Age, with frequent quotations from primary sources. Emphasis on the lives of the pirates and the individual captains who became famous, along with events that directly affected Virginia.

Frank Sherry, *Raiders and Rebels: The Golden Age of Piracy*. New York: William Morrow, 1986. A very readable account of the Golden Age. A former journalist, Sherry does an especially good job of drawing the reader into the events of the time.

Jo Stanley, ed., *Bold in Her Breeches: Women Pirates Across the Ages*. London: HarperCollins, 1995. A book of essays covering what little is known about female pirates through time; also concerned with the portrayal of women pirates in popular culture.

Alberto Teneti, *Piracy and the Decline of Venice 1580–1615*. Trans. Janet and Brian Pullan. Berkeley: University of California Press, 1967. Information on piracy in the Mediterranean shortly before the Golden Age.

Lloyd Haynes Williams, *Pirates of Colonial Virginia*. Richmond: Dietz Press, 1937. A short but informative book about piracy in early America.

Index

Picture Credits

About the Author

Stephen Currie is the author of more than thirty books and many magazine articles. Among his nonfiction titles are *Music in the Civil War, Birthday a Day, Problem Play, We Have Marched Together: The Working Children's Crusade,* and *Life in a Wild West Show.* He is also a first and second grade teacher. He lives in upstate New York with his wife, Amity, and two children, Irene and Nicholas.